TROPICAL
FISH
in
YOUR HOME

By Herbert R. Axelrod and

William Vorderwinkler

G. J. M. Timmerman, *Photographer*

STERLING PUBLISHING CO., Inc.   New York

WARD LOCK & COMPANY LTD.   LONDON

Contents

Revised Edition © 1960

Copyright, © 1956
by STERLING PUBLISHING CO.. Inc.
419 Fourth Avenue. New York 16. N. Y.
Manufactured in the United States of America
Library of Congress Catalog Card No. 56-7698

or Brocaded Barb . . . Cherry Barb . . . Sumatran or Tiger Barb . . . Stoliczka's Barb . . . Harlequin Fish or Rasbora . . . Dwarf Rasbora . . . White Cloud Mountain Fish

1. A Living Picture

Beautiful jewels of color and motion, graceful courtship amidst rich green plants, fascinating habits and exotic personalities—all in a single aquarium. That is reason enough for some 20 million people in America to maintain tropical fishes in their homes, but there are other reasons, too.

Doctors and dentists have long known the value of having an aquarium in their waiting rooms. It helps relax their patients and soothes their nerves. Some psychologists even prescribe the hobby for nervous people, or for those whose ailments require them to take long rests. Patients with eye trouble who must exercise their eye muscles have often been given an aquarium with some very active fishes, such as the Danio species, to watch. This has been found much less tedious and boring than long series of eye exercises, and has in most cases given better results.

The aquarium hobby is also a fascinating and simple approach to teaching natural history to children. Parents, instead of using the "birds and bees" lecture, which they often do not tell easily, can present the so-called "facts of life" in a natural and even fascinating manner by letting the children have an aquarium and a few pairs of inexpensive and colorful live-bearer fishes. More often than not, the parents too are ensnared by the charm of the fishes.

It is the purpose of this book to introduce you to the tropical fish aquarium, its inhabitants, its plants, and to the easy way in which it can be maintained.

SOME FALLACIES

There are many mistaken notions about aquarium keeping. Let us take up the prevalent ones, and see if there is any truth to them.

Fallacy Number One:

First of all, there is the fellow who looks at a large aquarium and says:

"What a lot of mess and bother it must be to change all that water!"

Well, if you had to, it would be. However, a properly kept aquarium need *never* be changed. True, there is a certain amount of evaporation which has to be compensated for now and then by adding fresh water. Naturally, if you wish to move the aquarium from one place to another, you must remove most of the water. If this is done, it is best to save the water that was taken out and put it back after moving. Changing water is done only in extreme cases: if the water has become fouled or is laden with disease bacteria, but generally not otherwise.

Fallacy Number Two:

"I wouldn't want one of those smelly tanks in my house!"

If they were smelly, no one would want them. An aquarium which gives off an unpleasant odor has something very much wrong with it—the result is that the water becomes foul. This may be due to a number of things, but about 90% of the time the fault lies with the misplaced generosity of the Lady (or Lord) Bountiful who dispenses the good things to eat. A fish can go a long time without being fed. Overfeeding to the extent that there is uneaten food left is a practice which is sure to bring on disaster, and quickly, too.

Fallacy Number Three:

"Aren't they beautiful! I'll bet they're awfully expensive!"

Wrong again! If they were expensive, would so many people be able to afford them? Most of the popular aquarium fishes can be bought for about 75¢ apiece. Some cost considerably less. True, there are a few rare species which represent a much bigger outlay, but these are the less attractive fishes. Here's how it works: a beautiful species of fish which is easy to breed is bound to be kept and bred by a great many people; the brisk demand for this beautiful fish is also the green light for the hatcheries to produce the species in large quantities. Suddenly this fish, beautiful as it is, becomes so commonplace that it is no longer a novelty, the demand lessens rapidly, and the price becomes ridiculously low.

The Neon Tetra, before people found out how to breed it, was a very expensive item imported from far up the Amazon. This little beauty, easily the most brightly colored of all aquarium fishes, is now bred extensively. A New York dealer recently offered them at a retail price of 5 for $1. Like all collectors' items, aquarium fishes are more apt to be priced according to their rarity rather than their beauty.

Fallacy Number Four:

"You can't keep those things! I had a friend who had a lot of fish and they died one after the other!"

This man's friend probably didn't believe in taking advice, either from a book or from someone who could tell him what he was doing wrong. You don't have to be a trained biologist, ichthyologist or any other sort of "-ologist" to maintain an aquarium successfully, and even be able to breed and raise most of the fishes available today. All you need is to follow a few common-sense rules, and your chances of success are almost certain. The thrill of seeing your fishes propagate under conditions which you provided is a never-ending source of satisfaction, one which never palls.

There are other fallacies which you may hear about aquarium keeping. Some of these might be hangovers from the days when the aquarist had much less equipment to work with, and when the equipment he had was much less dependable and more expensive. The fact still remains that the fish hobbyist has much more fun per dollar than any other hobbyist you could name. Many aquarists make enough profit on the surplus stock of fishes they raise to offset all expenses. How many people do you know with a hobby which pays for itself?

New York Zoological Society photograph by Sam Dunton

2. Setting Up the Aquarium

THE SHOW TANK

The kind of aquarium we are concerned with in this chapter is the show tank. This is an aquarium in which effort is made to create a beautiful background for beautiful fishes. The fishes are selected for their colors or other interesting characteristics, and the aquarium is to show them off to the utmost.

If several species of fishes are grouped, this becomes what is known as a "community aquarium." There are some fussy people who insist that, in order to conform with a true natural setting, you should confine your tank to fishes which are native to the same area. This gives a rather narrow scope, however, and most of us are likely to put together fishes from all corners of the globe, as long as they get along with each other.

There are some fishes whose beauty or interesting characteristics make them desirable in spite of their somewhat disagreeable habits when placed with strangers. These should be kept in separate tanks, if your interest in them is great enough to warrant keeping them at all.

UTILITY AQUARIA

There are special tanks also which are set up with a utilitarian purpose in mind. For instance, the hobbyist who wants to be sure he is not contaminating his aquarium with disease when new fishes are purchased will set up a "quarantine tank." Here he keeps his new purchases for a week or so. If the fishes remain healthy, he will then consider them safe to join the others.

Then there is the so-called "hospital tank" where fishes which contract disease are put in an effort to cure them.

Another type of aquarium is the "breeding tank." Here we set up conditions which will permit our fishes either to give birth to their young or to lay their eggs in the manner to which they are accustomed. Sometimes this breeding tank is not large enough to accommodate the youngsters when they begin to grow; they are then placed in a "raising tank."

The proper way to set up these utility aquaria varies, and will be taken up in the proper sections. However, we still have the community or show tank to consider, so let us proceed to a few pointers which will help in setting up aquaria in general.

PLACING AND LIGHTING THE TANK

In the first place, you must consider location. The ideal way to see a fish in all its colors is to have the sunlight shining on the tank from behind the observer. If it is at all possible to place your aquarium in such a location, and if the light is not too strong, you have perfection. Some of the color which you see when you look at a fish is refracted or bounced back; if the light is in a position where it will not bounce back, these delicate shades are lost. Remember, a diamond looks like a piece of glass unless it is held so that you can see its refracted colors.

Lighting the aquarium at night presents less of a problem. There are reflectors made to fit across the front of the aquarium, which come equipped with either incandescent or fluorescent lights. The incandescent lights are very satisfactory. Avoid getting the so-called "daylight" blue-tinted tubes if you purchase a fluorescent

Photo by Laurence E. Perkins, taken at Aquarium London

It is possible to use bog plants in an aquarium and have them grow out of the water.

fixture, as this gives a cold light which washes out many of the attractive blues and yellows in the fishes. There is a fluorescent tube known as "warm white" which will give a much better result.

Another thing you must check before filling the aquarium is whether or not it is standing level. The pressure is unevenly divided in a tilted aquarium, and leaks can be the result.

If you have a good, solid table for your aquarium, fine and dandy; if you decide to get yourself an aquarium of larger capacity, say 15 or 20 gallons, you will probably want to get a matching stand, which fits the bottom of the aquarium perfectly, and provides a good, solid foundation. A stand usually has the added feature of having a shelf underneath, where another aquarium may be added, if desired.

SHAPE OF THE TANK

There are torture chambers which come under the heading of "fish-bowls." Many thousands of these are still in use, many of them with goldfish in them, gasping at the surface for air. A bowl which bulges at the sides gives a smaller surface at the top than at the widest point, and is a trap for carbon dioxide gas. A fish breathes oxygen and gives off carbon dioxide, just as humans do, and when there is an oversupply of carbon dioxide, the fish is in trouble. Oxygen is absorbed by the water at the surface, but when the surface is small, the oxygen content of the water is greatly reduced.

The most sensible aquarium is a rectangular, metal-framed receptacle. This provides a water surface which is exactly even from top to bottom, and there are no curved glass surfaces to distort the shape of the fishes. You may be tempted to purchase an aquarium at a "bargain" price. This will get you an aquarium with a frame of thin, galvanized iron which has been painted; it may also have a weak, possibly flawed slate bottom. A tank like this may give satisfactory service for years, but sooner or later the paint will scratch off and give way to ugly rusty spots. A slightly higher outlay will give you a tank which has a stainless steel frame, a heavier slate bottom and better glass. Don't forget, you are buying something which will give you pleasure for many years.

This is the proper size gravel to use. If your gravel is too fine, it will not allow the plants to root properly; if too coarse, it will allow uneaten food particles to decay.

Photo by Mervin F. Roberts

GRAVEL FOR THE TANK

Now your aquarium is ready to be filled. Your first concern is to provide gravel as an anchor for the plants which you intend to use. A happy medium is called for here. If gravel which is too fine is used, the plant roots will have trouble pushing their way through it. On the other hand, if coarse gravel is used, fish detritus and un-eaten food will settle down through it resulting in foulness. A medium gravel, with grains about the size of the small "o" in this print, is about right.

Take enough of this gravel to cover an even inch of bottom, and pour it into a dishpan or a bucket. Set it where the receptacle can overflow and turn on your hose or faucet just enough so that you can push the nozzle or stream of water around in the gravel and loosen the dust-fine particles enough to overflow with the water. When the water comes clean, your washing chore is done. Pour the

After the gravel has been washed in a clean pail, pour it into an unfilled aquarium so you can mold it without stirring up the debris in the water.

Photo by Mervin F. Roberts

After molding the gravel, set in the rocks.

wet gravel into the aquarium, pushing it back from the front center so that it is deeper at the sides and back. There is a double reason for this: it gives deeper rooting for the plants, and secondly, all the trash will gather at the front, where it can be seen easily and removed by siphoning. When pouring the water in, place a sheet of white paper over the gravel and pour the water gently into a cup on the bottom, letting it overflow onto the paper, so as not to disturb the gravel, then remove the paper.

DECORATING THE TANK

Decorating is a matter of taste. In the old days, it was fashionable to put a lot of marbles, small castles, porcelain mermaids, and the like, into an aquarium. We still see many with decorations—divers, sunken ships, treasure chests—on the bottom. However,

The finished aquarium should look something like this . . . an imitation of nature.

most aquarists prefer to landscape or "aquascape" their tanks by creating a natural setting with rocks and plants.

You have a large selection of plants from all parts of the world to work with. A living picture can be created which equals any underwater scene in beauty. Of course, here again the purists might disapprove if the plants in one aquarium come from such varied places as Asia, Africa, Australia and South America. You can still create a lovely picture and limit your plants to those from certain areas, as well as fishes from the same areas. (More on this later.)

Where rocks are concerned, there are a few words of warning which must be heeded. A rock should not add anything to the water. Therefore those which contain minerals or those which are of a limestone nature will make the water very alkaline and are definitely "out." Rocks of a basaltic nature, or non-metallic rocks such as sandstone or granite, may be used safely. Here is a chance to give scope to your artistic ability by creating a background, using the rocks to set off the plants.

PLANTS FOR THE AQUARIUM

Your aim in setting up your aquarium is to try to imitate the natural surroundings of the fish you are keeping for pets.

In general, use the taller plants in back, and the shorter ones in the foreground, leaving an open space where the fish can show themselves.

Plant your aquarium when it is about one-quarter full of water. (If you already have your tank set up, remove some of the water and keep it in a container to add back later.) Push your rooted plants down so that the roots are well spread in the gravel and all buried. The unrooted plants should have the cut ends buried about one half inch in the gravel, where they will soon anchor themselves. Once the planting is done, add back the "aged" water by pouring it gently into an old saucer or cup standing in the open part of the aquarium. This will deflect the wash of the water upward instead of washing out the roots you have just buried and spoiling all your work.

Don't ever shock your tropical plants by using cold water! Temper it to about room temperature before pouring it in. Never add fresh water! It must always be aged. Water is too fresh if used out of the tap and will give much trouble, especially if it is chlorinated for drinking. Chlorine will kill fish and plants alike. Water, unless from a clean pond, must be allowed to set at least three days in some other container before it is used in the tank. This aging process may be speeded up with the help of tablets which de-chlorinate the water, available from most dealers.

SELECTING YOUR PLANTS

Different plants grow well in different types of aquarium settings. The depth to which they are planted, as well as the light they are to receive, is very important to consider before they are pur-

Cabomba caroliniana (fanwort) is a popular, low-priced aquarium plant, native to the southern states.

chased. Let's take a look at the various plants which are available for the home aquarium:

Cabomba caroliniana, commonly called simply "Cabomba," is native to the southern part of the United States. It is usually available at low prices from most dealers. Cabomba is a lovely plant that can be bunched with 5 or 6 strands. The fan shaped appearance of the leaves may have suggested its popular name, "Fanwort." This plant needs plenty of light and gets stringy when light is not available. If a tank is placed near a window where north light is always available during the daylight hours the plant will do very well.

When planting, snip off the bottom inch or so of the plants and place them about an inch into the sand so they may take root and not float up.

Elodea, or more scientifically, *Anacharis canadensis,* is another popular plant in home aquaria. This is one of the most common North American aquatic plants, and has been introduced in European waters. Cultivated plants are priced reasonably, are usually

Three kinds of *Myriophyllum* (milfoil), an excellent hiding grass for the new-born young of live-bearing fishes, and an excellent spawning medium for most egg-scattering fishes.

available, and will be found to be more attractive and grow better than wild plants.

Since *Elodea* and *Cabomba* grow to very long lengths under the proper conditions, it is wise to plant them to the rear of the aquarium so they will not grow in front of the smaller plants.

Milfoil, or *Myriophyllum spicatum,* is a plant closely resembling Fanwort, but is much more delicate in its lacy leaves. It, like all plants, will grow toward the light, so it is best to plant it in the back or on the sides of the aquarium where the most light is allowed to enter. It is fast-growing and is widely used to help egg-laying fishes to spawn. This plant has a wide distribution throughout the warmer portions of North and South America. Usually available at low prices.

Vallisneria spiralis is the most popular species of aquatic tape grass. It is native to the southern United States and is also found in Southern Europe. It grows very well in a moderate light, and when conditions are to its liking will propagate freely by sending out runners from the base. These runners take root at intervals and result in a whole series of new plants. Usually sold by the dozen at a moderate price. (See photo on page 20.)

Sagittaria natans resembles *Vallisneria,* but has wider, sturdier leaves. It is a little more difficult to grow, and propagates in the same manner as *Vallisneria,* but not as rapidly or as readily. Native to the southern United States, it is usually available at moderate prices.

The *Cryptocorynes* comprise a family which includes about 40 species of plants, some narrow-leaved, and some wide-leaved. They are native to the Malay Archipelago, and usually sell at a fairly stiff price. The reason is that these plants grow and propagate very slowly. This fact is offset by the beauty of these plants. Another item in their favor is that they grow best in about one-half the light required by other aquatic plants. When well established in condi-

Sagittaria (arrowheads) is available at moderate prices and is a beautiful plant with wide, sturdy leaves.

tions to their liking, these plants will live for years and propagate regularly by sending up shoots from their root-stock.

Echinodorus intermedius, or more commonly the Amazon Sword Plant, is an ideal center piece for a tank deep enough to maintain it. It is senseless to place an Amazon Sword Plant in a tank less than 12 inches deep. The plant will grow to 2 or 3 feet tall, depending on the depth of the water. It should be planted with the crown above the sand line and it sometimes needs to be weighted with a piece of lead until it roots.

It is truly the prince of aquarium plants and a good reproducer. The Amazon Sword Plant will make an attractive setting as it grows daughter plants all around it. When a runner starts going out, it is wise to weight the runner into the sand with a small rock or a piece of lead. The daughter plants may be severed from the parent plant as soon as they root.

As the name indicates, this attractive plant comes to us from the Brazilian Amazon region. It is usually available from most dealers, and prices vary according to the size of the plants.

A young Amazon Sword Plant.

This exceptional photograph shows a Neon Tetra swimming past the open flower of a *Cryptocoryne* plant. (Note the unopened blossom.)

This Corkscrew Val is a variety
of *Vallisneria spiralis* which has
leaves that curl around.

Some floating plants like *Lemna minor* and *Spirodela polyrhiza,*
the familiar Duckweed, are usually only a nuisance and should be
avoided. Sometimes they, as well as *Riccia, Salvinia, Utricula minor*
and *Eichhornia crassipes,* the Water Hyacinth, are used when one
is trying to encourage the fishes to spawn.

CARE OF PLANTS

Never use humus or soil of any kind to "fertilize" your plant-
ings. The fish will take care of that job. If the plants begin to lose
their green color and get stringy this simply means that they are
not getting enough light and more light should be offered them.

(Above) *Salvínia,* a floating plant. (Below) The proper method of planting rooted plants requires a half-full aquarium, or else your hand will cause an overflow.

3. Water

As we all know, water is composed of two parts of hydrogen, and one part of oxygen. This is water in its pure state, distilled water. In its natural state, there are many impurities mixed in, just as in the air we breathe. For our fishes, we must keep the impurities under control.

ACIDITY AND HARDNESS TESTS

There are two conditions of water which we are concerned with as aquarists. One is whether the water is acid, neutral or alkaline; the other is whether the water is hard or soft.

In order to determine acidity or alkalinity, there are several types of kits on the market known as pH kits. The usual kit consists of a small vial into which a sample of aquarium water is poured, and then dyed with a special preparation. The water is then compared with a color chart which goes from blue through green to yellow. Blue water shows alkaline, green neutral, and yellow acid. Fishes need neutral or slightly acid conditions.

Whether water is soft or hard can be determined roughly without the aid of a kit. If the water from the tap does not lather readily, or leaves a ring in the bathtub which is difficult to remove, you have hard water. Most fishes require soft water, so if your water is hard you must do something about it. But first you must know more exactly how hard the water is.

There are two types of test kits which determine the amount

of hardness in water. The simpler of the two consists of a graduated beaker and a bottle of liquid soap. A measured amount of aquarium water and a specified number of drops of the soap are placed in the beaker and the mixture is shaken up vigorously. The height to which the suds rise in the beaker is an accurate indication of the degree of hardness which the water has.

Another kit consists of three solutions and a small vial. The water to be tested is poured into the vial, and a specified number of drops of the first two solutions are added. This results in a deep purple solution. Then the third solution is added drop by drop. The water which was purple will suddenly turn blue, and the number of drops which it took to do the trick gives you the number of degrees of hardness of the water. The ideal aquarium water for all-around use should show no more than 10 degrees of hardness.

CONTROLLING WATER CONDITIONS

Suppose your water is hard and alkaline, as many tap waters are. You have one of two courses to choose: you can look for a natural source of soft water, such as an uncontaminated pond or brook, or you can correct your water artificially. If you seek a natural source, take your kit along, and make a test on the spot. A body of fresh water which has a fish population can be assumed to be fairly free of contamination.

There is another source of good aquarium water, and that is Jupiter Pluvius. Rain water is usually quite acid, and very soft. If you gather rain water, wait for a heavy fall, and do not catch it until it has rained for a while. The dust on a roof and in the air can be a real source of contamination, and should be allowed to wash away first. The rain water you finally collect should then be allowed to stand in a non-metallic container until clear. Then it can be separated from any settlings by pouring it off or siphoning it out. If a test shows that the resulting water is highly acid still, add alkaline tap water until the mixture is only slightly acid.

Recently, there came on the market a method by which hard water could be rectified artificially. One can now purchase a bag which contains a small quantity of acrylic resin crystals. This bag can be hung in the aquarium water for a few days until a test shows that the proper softness has been attained. For most fishes, between 5 and 10 degrees of hardness is proper. A few species require less or more for breeding. (These will be pointed out in their individual descriptions.)

You will probably find that as your water gets softer, it turns more acid. If it does not, it may be necessary to add a little acid solution. The least harmful, it has been found, is a brew made by boiling a handful of peat moss in about a quart of rain water and then allowing the result to settle. The boiling should be done in either an enameled or Pyrex container. The clear, dark-brown fluid can be bottled and kept indefinitely, and should be added to the tank water a little at a time until the proper acidity is attained. It may stain the water a light amber color, which is not unpleasant once you have become accustomed to it.

Adding tap water generally will turn your water to the alkaline side. You are aiming to get neutral or slightly acid tank water.

CHLORINE

Tap water usually contains some chlorine, which could do harm to your fish if they are added to tap water too soon. But chlorine soon leaves the water as it is allowed to stand, especially if the water is agitated by means of aeration or a filter. This is the big reason why water should be "aged" before putting fish into it.

In some districts, sodium fluoride is now being added to water as a means of preventing tooth decay. Here we have a double problem, that of getting rid of both the chlorine and the fluoride, which does not leave the water as a gas as chlorine does.

There are several chlorine and fluoride neutralizers on the market which do a good job chemically. These should be used where there is fluoridation, and may be used to speed up the de-chlorination process where there is only chlorine in the water.

When letting the water stand, be sure to use a wide-mouthed container. If a large bottle of the carboy type is used, fill it only to the point where it begins to narrow toward the neck. See

Page 14 for more on this subject in regard to plants and filling the tank.

OTHER IMPURITIES

Sometimes it happens that water will turn cloudy. A microscopic inspection will show that it harbors immense quantities of protozoan life. This sometimes happens in a newly set-up tank; however, it will clear up in a day or two. Protozoan life requires food, and in an empty tank this is rapidly exhausted and starvation clears them out.

Cloudy water in an established tank is a different matter. Here there must be a cause. The most common one is overfeeding; the uneaten food decays and provides sustenance for the swarms of protozoan life which cloud the water. A neglected tank with too much debris on the bottom is also very likely to develop this condition. A dead fish lodged somewhere out of sight can also be the culprit. In any case, the cure is the same: remove the cause. Siphon the decayed matter off the bottom and replace the water which was removed in the process with clean water. Dead fish, snails or plant leaves should of course be removed.

Cloudiness can be caused by infusoria, seen here magnified.

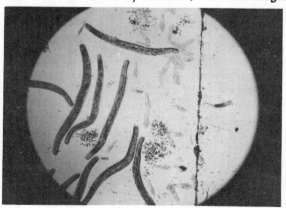

4. Aquarium Accessories

Now that you have the aquarium set up and ready for its finny occupants, you have to take stock of your other necessary equipment. In the first place, you will need a net. Don't get a very small one. One which is large enough to make fish-catching easy will save much wear and tear on the fishes, and on your own nerves.

An enameled pail is often very handy, as is a six-foot length of rubber or plastic hose. The pail is for transporting water, and the hose for siphoning water when you give your tank the occasional cleaning or change of water which it requires. If your aquarium is a small one, all you need for a satisfactory cleaning job is a dip-tube—a tube with a chamber on one end. You push down the chamber end to the bottom with your finger closing the upper end. Lifting your finger causes the water to rush into the chamber, carrying with it the dirt you want to pick up. Then you lift up the chamber and dump the dirty water into the waiting pail.

Certain fishes are adept at jumping out of the water. In order to curb this exuberance, you will find it necessary to cover the exposed top part of your aquarium with a piece of glass. If you are using a reflector with incandescent lamps for lighting, do not use a cover glass which extends all the way over the top. If the reflector is placed on top of the glass, a great deal of heat will be generated and the glass will crack. So, bring your glass up to the edge of the reflector. If you use a flourescent light reflector, much less heat will be generated, and you can put the reflector on top of the glass.

HEATERS •

The next problem is how to heat your aquarium comfortably for your fishes. This is usually no problem in the summer months, when there is heat aplenty. In the winter, however, we must provide our aquarium with an artificial source of heat. Before the days of electricity, tanks were heated by little lamps or gas flames under the base, and woe betide the aquarist who forgot to fill the lamp on a chilly night! Now we have dependable electric heaters with thermostatic controls which can be set so the water is heated to exactly the right temperature.

Heaters come in various wattages, for different sizes of aquaria. To figure the wattage required, multiply the gallon capacity of your aquarium by 5 watts; for example, a 10-gallon aquarium requires a 50-watt heater.

The over-all temperature range at which practically all tropical aquarium fishes are comfortable is 76° to 78°. This brings us to another piece of necessary equipment: an aquarium thermometer. This either floats in the water or is set on the bottom. (Do not expect an accurate reading from a floating thermometer which is near a light bulb.)

AIR PUMPS

Now we come to the question of whether or not to have aeration in the tanks. Consider the difference it makes, and then decide whether you want an air pump. Without aeration, a limited number of fish can be accommodated in your aquarium, averaging 2 inches of fish for each gallon of water. Now, what happens when you move this water by pumping a gentle air stream into it? The moving water immediately doubles its capacity to contain fish, because of the fact that a great deal more oxygen is now absorbed by the moving surface. Another thing also happens: the heat generated by the heater is distributed evenly throughout. Cool water has a tendency to be heavier, and without circulation in your tank, it might be several degrees cooler on the bottom than at the surface.

An air pump used to be a high-priced luxury. This is no longer the case; for a few dollars, you can get a model which works from a vibrator, and gives years of satisfactory service. If you have only one or two aquaria to be served, there is no need for anything more elaborate. If, however, you have grown to the point where you need air for a battery of aquaria, you will need a pump with a greater capacity, one which is powered by a motor and compresses the air with one or two pistons.

FILTERING

An air line lets you do one more thing: filter the water, and remove the unsightly suspended matter which sometimes prevents your water from being crystal-clear. There are many different types of filters, but they have only one job: to remove dirt. You do not need a large filter for a small aquarium, and a small one is not adequate for a large aquarium. A reliable dealer will be able to guide you here if you tell him your requirements.

All but the very largest filters work on the air-lift principle: a stream of air is pumped into a tube, where it is released in the form of a stream of bubbles. The bubbles traveling upward act as pistons and draw water with them. This water is replaced by other water rushing in, and a circulation is established.

The simplest type of filter utilizes the gravel in the bottom of the aquarium as a filtering medium. The air-lift tube ends in a plastic cup, which is buried in the gravel, and the water circulates into the tube from the surrounding gravel. The dirt which is drawn into the gravel quickly disintegrates when the water flows through it constantly, and the dissolved matter is in turn absorbed by the plants and fish, or dispelled at the surface. There are some variations on this type of filter. One type uses a perforated bed of plastic which covers the tank bottom under the gravel, and another uses a perforated plastic tube which goes all around the bottom. Still another draws the water through a porous plastic tube which is also buried.

Another simple filtering system has the air-lift tube draw the water into a plastic container which is perforated on top and filled with glass-wool. The dirt particles are trapped by the glass-wool and may be washed out when necessary. This filter rests on the bottom, but there is another type in which the box hangs at the surface and the dirty water is lifted into it; then it passes through the filtering medium and returns through perforations at the bottom.

A slightly more elaborate system uses the outside type of filter. Here the box with the filtering medium hangs outside the aquarium and does not take up any space inside the tank. There are two chambers, one with the filtering medium and the other empty. The wall between is perforated. A tube from the aquarium siphons the dirty water into the filtering chamber, and an air-lift tube returns the clean water into the aquarium.

Very large aquaria which require a brisk circulation of water sometimes use a filter which works on the inside filter principle but draws the water into the filtering medium by means of a tiny electric motor and pump.

In order to work efficiently, a filter must be prevented from becoming clogged. Clean it regularly. Glass wool may be removed and rinsed in running water until clean, and if the filter uses charcoal or gravel, a brisk rinsing under the tap will do the trick.

Here is a simple filter to keep your aquarium clear and clean.

5. Foods

Now that your aquarium is set up with its equipment, you can begin to turn your thoughts to what to feed your fishes.

Feeding is not a simple matter of shaking out a few grains from a box every day, as the fishes thrive and grow and grow. While fishes are far from being finicky where food is concerned, you just can't keep on feeding them the same things day after day, year in and year out. In the first place, no matter what the claims are on the box, no food is *that* perfect. In the second place, no matter how you like steak, you wouldn't want it exclusively every day in the week, would you?

Very few of us have the means at our disposal to give our fishes a varied diet of living foods every day, so the likelihood is that your aquarium fishes will get a prepared dry food of some kind. There are many of these foods on the market at the present time; practically all are very good, but none are perfect. They don't cost much. Buy three or four varieties, and then try varying these from day to day. If some are rejected, or consumed with reluctance, go easy on them, or throw them away. You will soon see what your fishes' preferences are, but don't narrow down to one food.

OVERFEEDING

The next paragraph should be in capital letters, because it is by far the most important piece of advice in this whole book:

Your fishes have a limited capacity for food, even though they are gluttons. When they have reached this capacity, they stop eating. Whatever food is left over spoils quickly, contaminating the water and providing sustenance for billions of harmful bacteria. If there is any food left on the surface or on the bottom 10 minutes after your fishes are fed, you are overfeeding. Avoid this and you will scarcely ever have any trouble with sick fish.

LIVE FOODS

Prepared fish foods are never a substitute for living foods; they are merely a supplement. True, some fishes can be kept in good health for a long time on an exclusive diet of dried foods. However, if you want to keep your fishes in really top-notch condition, you must give them an occasional meal of living food. Some of these foods are not difficult to come by; let us see what they are, and how we can provide them.

DAPHNIA: Although these look like insects, these little creatures are actually crustaceans, and lead a completely aquatic existence. They are red in color, and about the size of a pin-head. Swimming is performed in hops, and for this reason and their flea-like shape, they are often called "water-fleas." They occur in huge swarms in some bodies of fresh water which are rich in decaying vegetable matter, and have little or no fish population. If you are fortunate enough to be within traveling distance of one of these ponds, you have a valuable source of what is one of the best possible foods you can provide.

Daphnia do have the disadvantage of not keeping alive very long in a crowded state, however. Do not make the mistake of collecting too many, or you will have a foul mess when you get home. Collect only enough for about two generous feedings, and keep them in as large a container as you have on hand. Aeration helps to keep them alive.

For collecting, a fine-meshed net, preferably with a long handle, is required. A wire-meshed sieve is also useful, and a bucket of some kind with a lid. A little exploration will tell you where the heaviest concentrations of daphnia are to be found, and on a good day it should not take long to make your haul. A good frame for your daphnia net can be made by taking a crab-net and removing the netting. An old nylon curtain will provide good netting material. Sew a pocket of this material about a foot deep on this frame.

A screen on top of your tank should be used to sift the contents of the filled net as you empty it. This removes debris or insect larvae which would grow up in the aquarium and cause trouble. The screen should be coarse enough to allow the daphnia to swim through.

BOSMINAE: Some ponds will be found to contain an organism which is very similar to daphnia, but much smaller and black in color. These are bosminae, and are often found along pond edges. The swarms give the water the appearance of having black pepper suspended in it. This tiny food is just the ticket for baby fishes. They gorge themselves with it until they seem ready to burst.

MOSQUITO LARVAE: A walk through swampy terrain will sometimes disclose pools which are swarming with mosquito larvae; these swim with a wriggling motion, and spend a good deal of time on the surface, where they must come for air. A meal of these is just about the greatest treat you can give to your fishes, but too much generosity on your part with these will backfire: the warm water will speed up the larval growth, and every uneaten larva will result in a mosquito in your house.

ENCHYTRAE (WHITE WORMS): Here is a food which is excellent for your fishes, and can be raised with very little trouble. For this you require a wooden box about 2 feet square, with humus in it about 4 inches deep. Humus can be purchased at a garden supply store or nursery. In this box, place a culture of white worms, such as can be obtained from your dealer, if you do not have a friend with a box of worms going.

Moisten the soil slightly. This does not mean to make mud; just moisten the soil as you would for plants. A sheet of glass on top of the box will keep the soil from drying out, and will also permit you to see how things are going. To feed your worms, place a slice of wet white bread on top of the soil. This will disappear in a surprisingly short time, and turning over the soil will disclose the fact that the worms have multiplied. An old fork is a handy tool for this job, as it can also be used for removing the worms, which form balls. Another food which may be used with some success is boiled oatmeal (a couple of spoonsful). A friend of ours uses any left-over vegetables, and has some of the richest cultures of white worms we have ever seen.

For feeding worms to the fishes, a worm feeder is a handy piece of equipment. This consists of a cup of glass or plastic which is perforated in the lower area, and arranged to float on the surface. The worms wriggle through the perforations, to be gobbled up by the hungry fishes.

TUBIFEX WORMS: Many ponds which daphnia inhabit are also home for aquatic worms known as tubifex worms. These worms gather in clusters along the pond edges, where there is soft mud and a certain amount of decay. The clusters may be recognized by their bright red color. Gathering often proves to be quite a messy job, but if the worms are thick, the clusters may be felt as lumps in the mud and picked up almost intact. However, it is sometimes necessary to gather a whole bucketful of oozy, smelly mud in order to extract from it a handful of tubifex worms.

The easiest extraction process is performed by spreading about one-half inch of sand on the surface of the mud, and gently adding enough water to come one-half inch above the surface of the sand. It is then just a matter of waiting until the worms come up through the sand and form a cluster at the surface. Lift the worms out, and discard the mud and sand. You can keep the worms alive and healthy by placing them in a wide-mouthed jar under a cold-water faucet which has been opened enough to drip slowly.

For those who do not care to go to all this trouble, there are professional worm men who ship to most dealers, and a cluster can be bought at a pet shop at very little expense. The tubifex worms can be fed with a worm feeder in a similar manner to white worms.

BRINE SHRIMP (*Artemia Salina*): Here is what is doubtless the most convenient live food of all. Brine shrimp come to us in egg form, and are collected from two places, San Francisco and

Microphotograph by Dr. Cliff Emmens

Ogden, Utah. They are equally fine foods, the only difference between them being that the Utah eggs are a bit larger. The embryos remain dried up inside the eggs for an indefinite period of time, ready to hatch when placed in salt water. All you need do when you want a supply of living food is to follow the easy directions which come with the eggs. (These directions vary for the two types.) The newly hatched nauplii, which resemble very small daphnia, should be removed from the salt water in which they hatch by using a fine-meshed net. They will live for a short time in the fresh water of the aquarium. For obvious reasons, avoid pouring salt water into the fresh water when transferring the eggs.

There are other live foods which are useful for feeding to fishes. The larger species of fish may be fed chopped garden worms. Swatted flies and other insects are readily accepted.

There are also some substitutes for living foods which you should know about. When you come home from a successful fishing trip, give your pets a bit of fish roe or chopped-up fish liver which they will accept with enthusiasm. A piece of fish may also be frozen in the refrigerator, and an occasional meal provided by shaving off a slice with a razor blade and chopping it up into bite-size pieces for your fish. Shrimp, clams, oysters and other shellfish may also be used in this fashion.

6. The Secret of Spawning Fishes

"I don't know why it is, but Joe Smith seems to be able to spawn any fish he wants to!"

You will often hear this statement made by a fellow aquarist.

In the first place, an aquarist who says *he* "spawned" a certain species of fish is guilty of misstatement. What he should say is that a certain species of fish spawned *for him*. He may have helped by creating conditions which were to the fish's liking, but the credit for spawning still belongs to the fish.

No matter what favorable conditions you create, it will still do you no good if the fish you work with is not capable of reproduction. So your first task is to make sure of a few things.

The first thing is to find out whether you have a pair or not. This may sound silly, but a busy store clerk anxious to make a sale could easily be tempted to catch two immature fish and assure you that you are getting a pair, meaning a male and a female. Also, some fishes are difficult to "sex" (determine sex of) when full-grown, and impossible to sex when half-grown.

Another important thing is the *age* of the fish. Select a young, healthy couple in the prime of life. It is silly to expect good results from a feeble old pair of fish. Even a mature pair, new to your tank, may have trouble adapting themselves to the 'new environment, so avoid purchasing mature fish for breeding purposes.

Rather than choosing a large pair, try to get a half-dozen youngsters which are only half to three-quarters grown. You will then be in a position to observe them and become acquainted with their habits and food preferences. When they are ready for spawning, you may select the best specimens. In the case of Cichlids, you need not even select, as there is a tendency for males to pick females of their preference and "pair off." Your fish are almost certain to spawn in these cases.

THE "EASIEST" EGGLAYERS

Many aquarists who would like to try their hand at breeding egglaying fishes want to know which ones are easiest to breed. This always brings to mind an aquarium we once saw at an exhibition. The man had a 50-gallon aquarium, beautifully planted, into which he had put a few pairs of White Cloud Mountain Fish, *Tanichthys albonubes*. Beyond feeding them, he gave them no other attention, but in two weeks there were several hundred fish of all sizes swimming about in little schools. It was one of the high points of the show.

If you are looking for something almost as easy to breed, try one of the small Danios. The fry are very hardy, and easy to raise on prepared as well as live foods.

Most of the Barb family are easily spawned as well. If a well-conditioned pair are put together, things are almost bound to happen.

Once you have mastered a few of these fishes, you will be able to tackle some of the more difficult ones. Remember, good conditioning and proper attention to requirements are the two requisites which spell success.

THE BREEDING TANK

Any small, well-planted aquarium will serve as a "maternity ward" for live-bearing fishes. The female is put there when her bulging sides warn that her time is near. When her babies have all arrived, return her to the original tank, and let the youngsters get a start in the place where they were born. Larger quarters are then in order, where they will have plenty of room for growing. Of course, match the temperatures of the two tanks before transferring.

A breeding tank for egglaying fishes is a slightly more complicated thing. Here you must take the fish's breeding habits into consideration and plant or furnish the tank accordingly.

For fishes which spawn in bushy plants, such as most Barbs or Tetras, a tank of no less than 10 gallons for the smaller species, and 15 to 20 gallons for the larger ones, is recommended. Plant one side generously with *Myriophyllum* or *Nitella,* or if you prefer, a bundle of Spanish moss.

Cichlids usually require some rocks or similar retreats. Flower pots are often used, and are excellent. Dwarf Cichlids can be spawned easily in a 5-gallon tank, but the larger Cichlid varieties will require 15 to 20 gallons. Some of the really large ones like *Astronotus ocellatus* would require larger accomodations yet.

It is always advisable to let the youngsters get a start in the same tank where they hatch. Newly-hatched fry cannot stand any amount of moving; make sure the breeding tank is large enough so that they will not be crowded for the first few months, and leave them there. After this time they will be in much better shape for moving to other aquaria.

FISH PREFERENCES

Now we come to a point where you must observe and study your fish a little. Do your fish prefer to swim in the open, or are they always hiding? Do you find them in sunny spots, or do you have to look for them in dark corners? What is the nature of the terrain from which they come? Are they native to clear, running streams or sluggish, muddy-bottomed ponds? Do they come from far inland or from coastal waters?

How can you as an aquarist duplicate the conditions in which the fish feel at home? You cannot duplicate, but the conditions can be approximated.

First of all, keep in mind that a pond or stream does not resemble an aquarium. The glass sides let in a great deal of light where Mother Nature does not. Some fishes love sunlight, while others instinctively avoid it. Simple observation on this point will tell you whether it is better to select a bright or shady location for your spawning fish.

If you force a timid fish to show himself by taking away some of his hiding places, this increases his timidity and keeps him in a constant state of terror. How can a fish spawn under these conditions? It is better to provide such a fish with *more* plant thickets into which he can dodge. You may be surprised to see that he puts in an appearance more often when he knows that there are places where he *can* hide if something frightens him.

Fishes which are native to running streams, such as Danios or White Clouds, will not tolerate dirty water or very high temperatures. On the other hand, pond or lake dwellers, such as Cichlids, might pick a spot in shallow water near the shore for spawning, as Sunfishes do. Here the sun is bright and the water warm. In the case of other Cichlids, the presence of enemies forces them to hide in pockets along the shore, or in reed growths, or in rock piles. If you approximate these conditions, and make your fish feel at home, your battle for breeding is usually won.

As for the water itself, it will be found that a species of fish which comes from brackish, coastal water will require the addition of a little salt for its well-being. Rain-fed inland streams have an almost neutral, very soft water, while fishes from swampy regions require water of definitely acid character. They will survive without perfect water conditions, but they probably will not breed.

Don't be misled by the apparently careless procedure of the successful breeder who declares he has no trouble; just uses tapwater. There are all kinds of tap-water, and his kind may be just right for the fish he is breeding. He also is well aware of the other requirements of his fish, and supplies them too. Remember that the successful breeder will tell you of his successes; you don't often hear of his failures. Don't let failure discourage you; the "experts" have them too!

7. Diseases of Fishes

ANCHOR WORM (*Lernaecera* species)
Symptoms: Heavy whitish spots of curled-up, imbedded worms (actually this is not a worm but a crustacean).
Treatment: Remove with a sharp, fine needle. Paint spot with mercurochrome.

BLACK SPOT DISEASE (*Diplostomiasis*)
Symptoms: Spots are usually black, though in light-colored fishes the spots take on a brownish cast, and contain a slowly moving worm rolled up inside the cyst. The cyst is surrounded by heavily pigmented cells; thus the color symptom. In time the fish will be nearly covered with these parasites.
Treatment: Life cycle of this parasite is dependent upon a snail, though new fishes may carry it into an otherwise clean tank. Treat infected fish by adding 20 ml. of a 1:100 solution of picric acid and water to a gallon of water and bathing fish for an hour. You may remove the fish sooner due to distress.

CONSTIPATION
Symptoms: Loss of appetite, slight abdominal swelling, few, heavy feces.
Treatment: Soak dried food in medicinal paraffin oil, glycerin or castor oil. If fish refuses this food it must be taken off dried food diet and fed daphnia, mosquito larvae or Cyclops. *Do not use white worms* as they are a chief cause of constipation.

DROPSY (Caused by the basterium *Pseudomonas punctata*)

Symptoms: Bloating of the belly as though the fish were egg-bound.

Treatment: There is no known cure for dropsy. The antibiotics are of no value. Some suggest tapping the liquid from the body of the infected fish, but this is of little value.

EYE FUNGUS

Symptoms: This is a true fungus infection which might easily be fatal. The eye appears to be covered with a whitish scum; cottony appearance in later stage.

Treatment: Paint infected eye with 1% silver nitrate solution obtained from drugstore. (Tap water should not be used in mixing solution.) Then bathe fish's eye in a 1% potassium dichromate solution. The red precipitate which forms on the eye is harmless to the fish. The infected fish should be isolated in an aquarium containing 2 grains of potassium dichromate per gallon of water, until the eye heals, though the disease is not infectious.

FISH LOUSE (*Argulus foliaceus*)

Symptoms: An external visible parasite about as large as a Daphnia, it attaches itself to the skin of the host by two suckers and lives off the blood sucked from the host.

Treatment: Parasite may be removed with a pair of forceps or tweezers and the spot painted with mercurochrome or peroxide of hydrogen. If parasites are difficult to remove, touch them with a piece of salt.

FLUKE (*Gyrodactylus and Dactylogyrus*)

Symptoms: Fish loses color and grows pale, fins close, skin becomes slimy and small blood-spots appear on the body and base of fins. Breathing is more rapid.

Treatment: Treat fish with 5 drops of 5% methylene blue per gallon of water or a 1:100 formalin-water solution. Use aeration when treating with formalin.

A pair of Astyanax infected with fungus.

FUNGUS INFECTION (*Saprolegnia*)

Symptoms: A cottony growth about a single or multiple site. Area usually will first show signs of being bruised or torn, as fungus cannot attack a healthy fish.

Treatment: Paint infected areas with a diluted (1:10 solution of commercial strength) preparation of either iodine or mercurochrome. Entire aquarium may be treated with a 1% potassium dichromate solution, or 1 gram of crystalline potassium dichromate to 7½ gallons of water. After fish is cured water should be changed. Treatment should last about a week.

ICH (*Ichthyophthirius multifiliis*)

Symptoms: White spots of pinhead size pepper the body and fins of the fish. Fish gets sluggish, closes fins, and gradually dies.

Treatment: Ich is a parasite which cannot be treated while still in the skin of the fish. Raising the water temperature will hasten

This Scat has the Ich.

the departure of the ich from the host for reproductive purposes. Then you can easily get rid of it. Use 50 mg. of quinine hydrochloride per gallon or bathe infected fish in a brine bath, 4 tablespoons of salt per gallon of water. Leave fish in either bath for at least 3 hours *after* each fish is clean of white spots.

KNOT or PIMPLE DISEASE (*Morbus nodulosus*)

Symptoms: Not really a specific infection but rather a series of parasitic sporozoa. Looks like Ich but is really little knots, or pimples. "Stubborn Ich" might well be name of this disease.

Treatment: No known cure. Remove infected fish immediately and treat for Ich. If this treatment fails, infected fish should be destroyed.

LEECH

Symptoms: External parasite visible as it is attached to the host, sucking its blood.

Treatment: Place the infected fish in a 2½% salt solution for ½ hour. Remove remaining parasites with forceps and paint area with mercurochrome.

LOSS OF COLOR

Symptoms: Fish becomes pale and its colors are not sharp. Normally active live-bearers lose sexual interest.

Treatment: This is strictly a food problem. The diet deficiency is due to a monotonous, unbalanced diet. Feeding of tubifex, daphnia and other live foods usually remedies the situation within 24 hours.

NEON TETRA DISEASE (*Plistophora hyphessobryconis*)

Symptoms: Blemish or spot forms along the "neon" blue-green line on Neon Tetras and related species. As disease progresses the area becomes extended.

Treatment: No known cure, though treatment with 500 mg. *each* of terramycin and aureomycin per 15 gallon aquarium helps considerably.

POP-EYE; EXOPHTHALMIA

Symptoms: The eye starts to bulge as though it were being forced out by an accumulation of fluid behind it.

Treatment: Antibiotics are of no value. No known cure. May be caused by *Pseudomonas punctata* (dropsy).

SCALE PROTRUSION (Either *Mibrio piscium* or *Bacterium lepidorthosae*)

Symptoms: Scales of fish start to protrude all over the body. Fish moves slower, frequency of breathing increases, tail becomes paralyzed and fish stays near top of water.

Treatment: As soon as scales begin to protrude, treatment should begin. Aureomycin, 250 mg. per gallon of water helps at times, but isn't a "sure cure." There is no known absolute remedy. Once this infection has been observed all members of the infected tank should be sterilized by adding 2½ grains of potassium dichromate and two teaspoonsful of salt to each gallon of water. Change water completely after two weeks.

SLIMY SKIN DISEASE (*Cyclochaete domerguei*) (*Chilodon cyprini*) (*Costia necatrix*)

Symptoms: There is a slimy secretion seen on the fish's skin. The fish loses its color, grows paler as the slime covers the entire outside of the fish.

Treatment: 30 minute bath in a 2½% salt solution; repeat in 48 hours, and every two days after that until all symptoms are gone. At least three known organisms are responsible for the symptomatic slimy skin disease. If the salt treatment fails, 2 grains of quinine hydrochloride should be added to a gallon of water and the infected fish should be maintained in this treated water until it is cured. A bath in 2 ml. of formalin per gallon of water, for 15 minutes is a last-resort treatment.

SPOTTINESS OF THE SKIN IN LABYRINTH FISHES (*Pseudomonas fluorescens*)

Symptoms: Whitish or bloody patches appear on the skin and fins of the infected fish.

Treatment: There seems to be no known cure for this disease. *Pseudomonas* seems to thrive in an antibiotic environment. Since labyrinth fishes are usually involved, a high temperature plus a heavy salt bath might work, though it has shown positive results in only few cases out of many. Try 90° F. for 2 hours in a 5% salt solution.

SWIM BLADDER DISEASE

Symptoms: Fish has difficulty swimming. It falls head-over-tail or cannot maintain itself on an even level in the water. May rest on the bottom.

Treatment: Not a fatal disease, but crippling. Fish seldom recovers. It is caused by physical factors such as poor diet, chilling, sudden changes of temperature or pressure.

TAIL-ROT AND FIN-ROT, often called TAIL-FUNGUS, MOUTH FUNGUS.

Symptoms: None of these are true fungus infections. They are caused by slime bacteria and are easily seen by the whitish appearance of the infected area. The sooner the disease is observed the easier it is to cure. Water changes are often responsible for weakening the fish's resistance to bacterial infections of this sort.

Treatment: Aureomycin is ideal for treatment. Single fish may be treated with a 10 mg. tablet of aureomycin in a quart of water. Entire aquarium may be treated with a dose of 250 to 500 mg. of aureomycin per gallon. Sometimes cures are effected with a 500 mg. dosage per 15 gallons of water, but this only removes the symptoms while the cure is in doubt. Bathe the fish in a strong salt solution after the aureomycin treatment. Use 4 tablespoonsful of salt per gallon.

TUBERCULOSIS

Symptoms: Loss of appetite, sluggishness, progressive thinness and gradual wasting away. Yellow spots at the base of the caudal peduncle in Tetras are also a sign.

Treatment: Treatment with streptomycin and PAS (para-amino-salicylic acid) are possible cures in the early stages. 10 grains per gallon of water is the recommended dosage. Prolonged overcrowding might be the cause of this disease. No "sure cure" known.

VELVET DISEASE (*Oodinium limneticum*)

Symptoms: May resemble Ich, but a closer look will show smaller spots, which, when viewed from reflected light, have a velvet-like appearance on the fish's skin. Often the skin looks as though it were peppered with fine powder. White Clouds seem especially susceptible to this disease.

Treatment: Add 2 drops of 5% methylene blue solution per each gallon of aquarium water. Acriflavine, same strength, may be substituted for methylene blue. Keep tank in complete darkness. Remove and sterilize, or throw out, plants. Treatment lasts for 5 days; then a 3-day rest and complete water change, then another treatment.

8. Fishes for the Aquarium

Now that we have learned how to set up our aquarium and how to take care of our fishes, let us turn to the all-important subject of what the available fishes are, what individual requirements they might have, and how they may be propagated.

HISTORY OF AQUARIUM FISHES

The world of aquarium fishes is a large one. Time was when, not so long ago, there were very few fishes brought into the country, for the simple reason that, although there was a demand, there were not many collectors. The German aquarists took a great deal of the initiative in this field, and got a number of sailors and ship captains to pick up fishes at the seaports where their boats docked. When a few precious specimens were gotten in this manner, every effort was made to mate them. Many of our early favorites were obtained from the offspring of these fishes. When it was finally realized that there was so much of a demand for exotic aquarium fishes, there were several large fish importing companies organized, and many fishes which were hitherto unobtainable were made available to the hobbyist; many species owe their continued existence to the efforts of hobbyists who after an intensive study of the habits of certain fishes, were able to solve the riddle of how they bred and made greater numbers of these otherwise rare fishes available. In spite of these, there are still some fishes which have rarely or never bred yet while in captivity. One of the most fascinating facets of this hobby is to get to work on these "difficult" fishes and get results. However, for the aquarist who is content to take the easier ones and get the satisfaction of seeing young fishes in his aquaria which he raised, there are many species which are not very finicky in their requirements and will spawn readily if given half an opportunity. It would take a heavy volume to present to you all the fishes which it is possible to keep and breed in aquaria. You might devote half your life to getting out a complete work on all aquarium fishes known to the fish world, and then find that by the time the book was published there were a score or more newcomers brought in; you just can't keep up with them!

There has been no effort made at completeness in this book; the fishes described here are available everywhere from time to time. Many are in constant supply. If you find that you have a fish which is not listed here, you will usually find that the general requirements for his family will fit him quite well.

FISH PRICES

There has always been a widespread belief among those who are uninitiated in the aquarium hobby that tropical fishes are expensive, as well as difficult to keep. Nothing could be further from the truth. The newcomer generally gets his biggest surprise when he finds out how inexpensive most fishes are.

The greatest paradox in aquarium fish prices is the best-known fish of all: the Guppy. A common Guppy can be bought for a few cents, while a pair of fancy, line-bred show Guppies may bring astronomical prices, if they can be bought at all. A price of $25 per pair is not unusual.

There is a reason for this: a good strain of Guppy takes a long time to produce. There is a great deal of inbreeding, and much unsatisfactory stock must be culled out and disposed of. Before a breeder has something which will command top prices, he must spend a lot of time and do a lot of work.

Other live-bearing fishes are comparatively inexpensive. Prices vary with the size and quality of the stock, but a dollar bill or less will generally buy a pair of live-bearers, with the possible exception of large Black Mollies, which come a little higher.

With the egglaying fishes, prices vary considerably, but practically all of the easily bred species can be purchased considerably under a dollar each. This group would include the Danios, Barbs, many of the Tetras, the young of most Cichlids, many of the Catfishes, and others.

Some fishes are not so easy to breed, grow slowly, or require other special attention. The Siamese Fighting Fish, for instance, presents a problem for breeders. In order to keep the beautiful, flowing fins of the males intact, it is necessary to raise each fish individually in its own glass jar. This requires a great deal of shelf space, as well as cleaning of the jars and feeding individually. The breeder gets (and deserves) a slightly higher price for this reason.

Other fishes, such as the Cyprinodonts, also present problems. The eggs take about two weeks to hatch, and each female will lay only a few eggs per day. The result is that you get a group of young which varies greatly in size and must be sorted frequently to prevent the big ones from eating the little ones. This is extra trouble for the breeders, who seldom bother with them. Therefore, if you should be shopping for some *Aphyosemion, Epiplatys, Pachypanchax, Aplocheilichthys,* or similar species, you will probably find them a bit expensive, if you find them at all.

Then there is another group of fishes which may be a bit higher priced than the average: these are the fishes which are seldom, if ever, spawned in captivity. In order to have these in supply, the dealer must import them from the country to which they are native. Air freight over long distances is an expensive proposition, and losses among wild fishes are much greater than with tank-raised specimens; you have to pay for this.

Family *Poeciliidae*

This is the family of live-bearing Tooth-Carps which includes the well-known Guppy, Platy, Swordtail and Molly. These species usually introduce the aquarist to the world of fishes. Keeping and breeding them is usually a simple matter of putting a healthy male and female together and waiting for Nature to take its course. The bulging abdomen of the female is the signal for her to be moved to a maternity tank, which should be heavily planted to give the newly-born young plenty of places to hide from their mother, who might easily mistake them for edible tidbits.

By means of selective breeding, it has been possible to produce many beautiful strains. This is where the amateur aquarist can compete with the professional breeder by producing strains of his own.

The usual method of selective breeding consists of starting with a pair that is as desirable as possible physically and color-wise. Then you sort out the offspring, culling out the runts as quickly as they prove to be inferior. As soon as they begin to show signs of becoming males, the selected youngsters should be separated, until nothing but females are left in the breeding tank. The best of the second generation females are then mated back to their father, and then there is a fairly well-established strain.

By the time the offspring of the father-to-daughter mating grow up, it will be obvious what the males from this mating look like. There is a fairly good chance that one of these males will be an improvement over his father. He will be the logical candidate to be mated to a virgin female of the last mating. This may seem to be inbreeding of the worst kind, but it is surprising how much inbreeding a healthy strain of fish can stand before there is any evidence of degeneration. The important thing is to use only the *healthiest* specimens from each generation.

Genus *Lebistes*

The Guppy, *Lebistes reticulatus* Peters

The original members of this family came from Trinidad, but the beautiful present-day specimens are a far cry from their ancestors. Here we are able to see the results of selective breeding in its most varied form: short fins, long, flowing fins, lace fins, reds, yellows, blues, swordtails, double swordtails, lyretails, round tails, veiltails, scarftails and many others. Whenever further possibilities seem exhausted, someone manages to come along with a strain which is even more beautiful than the rest.

The Guppy is one of the hardiest of fishes; it demands nothing more than fairly clean water, and a temperature of 76°. It thrives in the smallest aquarium, and a healthy female thinks nothing of giving birth to as many as 60 or 70 offspring. Feeding is no problem; it is fond of living foods, but is also satisfied with the prepared ones.

Keep some plant life in their aquarium; they enjoy nibbling at plants, but do not damage them. All they are after are the minute algae which grow on the leaves. They are active little creatures, always on the alert. Unfortunately, most of the colors are lavished on the males. The females are comparatively drab, olive green in color, some with a bit of black marking in the tail.

Genus Mollienisia

The Sailfin Molly, Mollienisia latipinna Le Sueur
(*See color photo on page 70.*)

One of the few live-bearing fishes native to our own United States is the Sailfin Molly. It is quite large, attaining 4 inches in length, and the big, beautiful dorsal of the male makes it unmistakable. The sides of the body carry from 6 to 8 rows of green dots, which extend into the tail, and the male has a huge dorsal fin which has a reticulated pattern on the lower half, while the upper half is covered with green dots.

Most people have trouble keeping this fish; there is a great temptation to put it into the community aquarium, but the sad fact is that water which suits the others does not suit the Molly. Being a large, active fish, the Molly needs plenty of room plus a temperature of about 78°. Being primarily a salt-water fish, it requires some salt in the water: a teaspoonful of Epsom salt and two of table salt per gallon is perfect. The third requirement is a partly vegetable diet. An occasional meal of chopped spinach is welcome. When the females become pregnant, they should not be moved to the maternity tank too late; this often causes premature birth.

There is a black color variety of this fish which has come

to overshadow the green forebears in popularity, and for good reason. A fully grown, velvety black male with its big dorsal fin is a gorgeous thing. Whether green or black, however, the Molly has the same special requirements.

Genus *Xiphophorus*

The Swordtail Helleri, *Xiphophorus helleri* Heckel

Another of the popular live-bearing species is the Swordtail. The male is distinguished by an unusual tail formation, the lower caudal rays being greatly elongated into a sword-like point. The female has almost as much color, but no sword. Top size for tank-raised females is about 4½ inches, with the males about an inch shorter. The sides are bluish green, with a red horizontal stripe running the length of the body through the center. In the male, this stripe extends as the upper edge of the sword. There is another horizontal stripe which runs from the belly to the tail, and extends as the lower edge of the tail in the male. The middle stripe is edged with gold, and the dorsal fin is peppered with red dots. A peaceful fish, it is a favorite for the community aquarium. It is a jumper, and the tank should be kept covered.

The Swordtail has been successfully crossed with the Platy, resulting in many interesting color combinations. There is also an albino form, which is light pink in color where the common fish is green, and a brownish red where the red colors appear in the green form. These fish have pink eyes, and there is now a new color variation which has been produced by breeding the albinos back to a red variety, resulting in a beautiful blood red albino with red eyes. There are many hybrid variations which have been produced by crossing the Swordtail with different color varieties of the Platy, resulting in such fishes as the Red, the Red Wagtail, the Tuxedo, the Variegated, and many other types of Swordtails. All are attractive, and all are peaceful and hardy.

The Platy, *Xiphophorus maculatus* Gunther

The Platy is another of the very popular family. It is native to Mexico, like its preceding relative, the Swordtail. A large female would measure 3 inches, and the male is considerably smaller. The original forebears of this family resemble very little the highly developed breeds now available. They are a muddy-colored brownish fish, with a few blue patches and a red spot here and there. By selective breeding, many color varieties have been produced, such as the Red, Black, Blue, Tuxedo, Gold Wagtail, Red Wagtail, Gold, Berlin, Salt-and-Pepper, Bleeding Heart, and others. This fish has been found valuable in cancer research; scientists have been able to develop strains which have cancerous tissues, and have thereby been able to make a close study of these tissues in a living animal.

The Platy is very peaceful and desirable in the community aquarium. If you wish to use Platies for selective breeding, remember that they will interbreed if put together, and one fertilization will produce anywhere from 4 to 7 batches of offspring.

The Variegated Platy, *Xiphophorus variatus* Meek

This is one of the originally colorful members of the family. It did not require much selective breeding to produce the colors known today. The most popular color variety, known also as the Sunset Platy, has a light blue body, shading to yellow on the belly. The dorsal fin is a bright canary yellow, and the tail is a bright red. The female is muddy color throughout, with nothing but a brown horizontal line to relieve the monotony. Possibly the reason for a slight apathy on the aquarist's part where this fish is concerned is the fact that the males do not begin to get their pretty colors until they attain maturity. Otherwise they are a peaceful, attractive and prolific fish.

Family *Cyprinidae*

These are the carp-like fishes of the world, of which many of the smaller members make excellent aquarium inhabitants. They come from all continents except Australia, and strangely enough, South America.

Genus *Brachydanio*

The Pearl Danio, *Brachydanio albolineatus* Blyth
(See color photo on page 67.)

Pearl Danios are among the most active of aquarium fishes. They are always scurrying about busily, in search of food or each other, and will add a great deal of life to any community aquarium. They are responsible for a great amount of profanity on the part of anyone who has tried to catch a desired individual in a well-planted aquarium.

A small, slender fish, the Pearl Danio never exceeds 2½ inches in length. Its sides are of a mother-of-pearl iridescence, and the specific name "albolineatus," meaning white-lined, is a misnomer. The fish was originally named from preserved specimens which showed a white horizontal line but actually this line is orange in color.

Here is a good fish for anyone who wants to try his hand at breeding egglayers for the first time. An all-glass aquarium of one to two gallons capacity is covered with pebbles or glass marbles on the bottom, and then fresh tap water is added to the depth of about 3 inches. This is allowed to stand for a day, and then a heavy female and two healthy males are added. Almost at once a wild chase begins, and eggs are scattered all over. Eggs are non-adhesive, and drop down between the pebbles. When the female is depleted, the parents are removed. The eggs may be seen by placing a light above the pebbles and looking up through the glass bottom. Hatching takes place in 48 hours, and the young become free-swimming in another 48 hours, when they may be fed with fine foods. Temperature, 76° to 78°.

This fish is native to Sumatra, Burma and Thailand.

The Zebra Danio, *Brachydanio rerio* Hamilton-Buchanan

From India comes the most popular of the group, the Zebra Danio. Like the Pearl Danio, it is 2 inches in length, and just as active. The body is silvery, with wide blue horizontal stripes running from the gill-plate all through the sides, the tail, and even the anal fin. Fullness of body is not an infallible guide to sex; a depleted female can look just like a male. However, the background on the anal fin of the female is silver, and on the male, gold.

Breeding procedure is exactly similar to that for the Pearl Danio.

The Spotted Danio, *Brachydanio nigrofasciatus* Day

This smallest member of the family, 1½ inches in length, comes from Burma. The sides are adorned with several greenish-blue stripes across the upper half of the body, and rows of spots on the lower half. It is as active as the others, and may be spawned as easily in the same manner as *B. albolineatus*.

(*See photograph on top of next page*)

(Above) The Spotted Danio, described on page 56. (Below) The
Danio Devario, described on page 58.

Genus *Danio*

Danio devario Hamilton-Buchanan

This is a rare fish, and probably for that reason it has never been tagged with a popular name. It comes from northern India, and reaches a length of 4 inches. The sides are steel-blue above and silvery below. Three deep blue bands run from the middle of the body to the caudal base, where they converge to form a blue stripe which runs into the upper half of the tail. (See photo on p. 57.)

A tank of at least 10 gallons with a clump of bushy plants at one end is required for breeding this large, active fish. The water should be partly fresh with a temperature of 80°. Hardness and pH do not seem to matter. The pair swim in and out of the plants, stopping side by side every once in a while to deposit eggs in the plants. The young are quite large and easily raised.

The Giant Danio, *Danio malabaricus* Jerdon

For all its size, the Giant Danio will not molest any fish it cannot swallow. The size is a respectable one for an aquarium fish: 6 inches. It comes from the western coast of India as well as Ceylon.

The body is blue, with a few short vertical bars just behind the gill-plate. From here back to the tail, there are two yellow horizontal stripes. The fins are orange in the female, and almost red in the male.

Breeding this large, active fish takes a tank of at least 20 gallons. Otherwise, the procedure is similar to that for the *Danio devario*.

Genus *Puntius*

This genus includes a great number of fishes. For a long time, the generic name was known as *Barbus* and this name, although incorrect, will probably stick for a long time. This large family ranges in size from the 6-foot Mahseer of India to the tiny Golden Dwarf Barb, *Puntius gelius,* which rarely attains a length of 2 inches. Most of the Barbs are peaceful; they are valuable aquarium fishes because in addition to their beauty, they have excellent appetites and prefer to feed on the bottom and clean up a lot of food which would otherwise spoil.

All conform to the same breeding pattern, and if you find that you have a Barb in your possession which is not listed here, the only thing to remember is, if it is large, it requires a large aquarium; the smaller species will spawn in a smaller space.

The Rosy Barb, *Puntius conchonius* Hamilton-Buchanan
(*See color photo on page 66.*)

This is one of the medium-sized Barbs, which is fully grown at 4 inches. It occurs in India, and its disposition is peaceful. Normally, it is a silvery, large-scaled fish with a black spot near the caudal peduncle. The males are a bit slimmer, and the fins just a shade darker than those of the females, whose fins are plain. At breeding time, however, a great change takes place: the male's entire body becomes suffused with a deep rose-pink color, and the fins become black. Young, immature specimens never show these colors, and when a male gets them it is a good indication that he is ready for spawning. Put him with a female whose sides are well rounded and you can be fairly sure of success.

A tank of about 15 gallons is right, and a temperature of 80°.

The tank should be well planted on one side with thickets of bushy plants. When conditions are right, driving begins shortly, the male trying busily to coax and cajole the female into the plants. Her coyness soon disappears and they swim into the thickets together, occasionally stopping side by side and quivering as about 4 to 6 eggs are dropped to be fertilized at once by the waiting male. This Barb is prolific, and 300 to 400 fry from one spawning is not at all unusual. Hatching time is a little under 2 days, and the fry absorb their yolk-sacs in another 2 days. At this time they must be fed. Be guided by the amount of fry as to the amount of food given.

The Clown Barb, *Puntius everetti* Boulenger

Many people who buy this Barb when still young, at a size of 1½ inches or so, are astonished when they see how big it gets. Five inches is not an unusual length. The fish is gaily colored, the sides being rosy pink and the fins red. A large round deep purple spot is found at the exact center of the side, from which an indistinct horizontal line extends to the tail base. There is a saddle on the shoulder, and another halfway between the dorsal fin and the tail. At the base of the dorsal fin there is another dark area.

To breed this large member of the family you need an aquarium of at least 20 gallons. Planting should be quite heavy, and the breeders separated for a few weeks and heavily fed. When the female bulges with eggs and the male is highly colored, put them together and raise the temperature to 80°. There should be no further difficulty. Other instructions coincide with those for the Rosy Barb.

The Striped or Zebra Barb, *Puntius fasciatus* Bleeker

This rare, attractive Barb has seldom if ever been bred. It comes from Sumatra and Borneo; the fish is gold in color, and there are 4 black stripes. The first ray of the dorsal fin is also black. The length is about 4 inches.

Here we have a fish on which the aquarist can try his skill at breeding. The full-size specimens available seem healthy and in good shape. Perhaps some water condition in their habitat which must be duplicated, or some item of diet supplied. This fish would certainly be a desirable addition to any collection if it became generally available.

Black-Spot Barb, *Puntius filamentosus* Cuvier and Valenciennes

Like the Clown Barb, this is one of the big ones; 7 inches is usually the full size. Half-grown specimens are particularly attractive. The sides are golden, with an indistinct band vertically just in front of the dorsal fin, and a large black spot halfway between the dorsal fin and the tail. The dorsal fin is red, as well as the outside rays of the tail, which are tipped with black. As the fish becomes older, the colors fade somewhat.

When the male is ready for spawning, his face becomes covered with sexual tubercles, which resemble pimples. The female makes apparent her readiness for spawning by bulging with eggs.

Spawning is similar to the *Puntius everetti,* and results are sometimes astronomical. When broods are large, they should be spread out to extra tanks as they grow, to prevent excessive crowding.

The Golden Dwarf Barb, *Puntius gelius* Hamilton-Buchanan

In contrast to the larger Barbs here is the "baby" of the family. Although a maximum size of 2 inches is given for this fish, it seldom exceeds 1½ inches. The male is a bit smaller than his mate, who has the fuller shape. The Ganges River, India, is its home. It does not have the short, plump shape found in most Barbs but more closely resembles the Rasboras. The body color is olive green, with black spots near the caudal peduncle and at the base of the dorsal fin and anal fin.

A few extra precautions must be taken with the aquarium when spawning this little fellow. A 5-gallon tank is ample. The bottom should be covered with pebbles or glass marbles, as well

as the bushy plants otherwise used. The parents are extremely fond of their own caviar, but many of the eggs fall to the bottom; hence the pebbles.

Spanner or "T" Barb, *Puntius lateristriga* Cuvier and Valenciennes

This is another of the large Barbs. It comes from a wide range which includes Java, Borneo, Sumatra, Malaya and Thailand. It attains a size of 8 inches and requires so much space that it is not often bred in aquaria.

There are no startling colors, but the pattern is unique; the background is olive, with a slight pinkish tinge in the fins. There are two vertical black bars, one just behind the head and the other at the front half of the dorsal fin. Connected with this posterior bar is a black horizontal line, giving the appearance of the letter "T" lying on its side. The British hobbyists use a little more imagination and see the horizontal line as the handle, and the two vertical bars as the jaws of a monkey wrench or "spanner," as it is called in England. These colors fade as the fish grows older.

If you have a large enough aquarium and wish to try spawning them, the "T" Barbs follow the same pattern as the others.

(Above) A trio of Cherry Barbs. (Below) A pair of Checkered Barbs, *Puntius oligolepis.*

(Above) The familiar Rosy Barbs, *Puntius conchonius*. (Below) A pair of Clown Loaches.

(Above) Pearl Danios. (Below) The Panchax (Aplocheilus) lineatus.

(Above) The Bumblebee Fish. (Below) The Penguin Fish, *Thayeria sanctae-mariae* Ladiges.

(Above) The Red Jet Swordtail. (Below) An Albino Swordtail.

(Above) The Green and the Black Sailfin Molly. (Below) The Blue Gularis.

(Above) The majestic Angelfish, *Pterophyllum* species. (Below) The Discus
Fish.

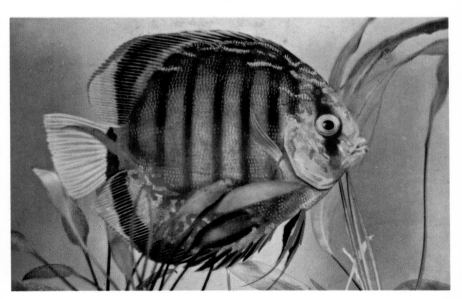

(Above) A trio of beautiful *Hyphessobrycon rosaceus*, the Rosy Tetra, a fish closely related to the *Hyphessobrycon callistis*, the Jewel Tetra (below).

(Above) *Pelmatochromis kribensis* and (below) *Apistogramma ramirezi* are both desirable Dwarf Cichlids.

(Left) Dwarf Gouramis in a spawning embrace. The two Pearl Gouramis (below) are peaceful fish for the community aquarium.

(Above) The Fire-Mouth Cichlid. (Below) The Banded Cichlid, or Convict Fish.

(Above) The *Betta splendens*, Siamese fighting fish, in a mating position, with the golden fish, the male, forcing eggs from the female.

The male catches the eggs in his mouth before they hit the sand.

(Above) After catching the eggs, the male spits them into his prepared bubble nest.

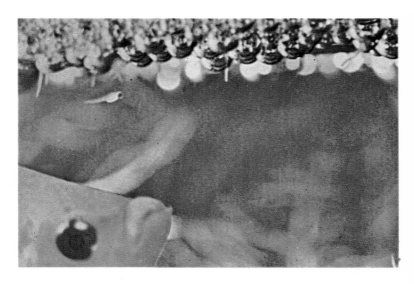

The male guards the young until they are free swimming. Note the fry, just hatched.

(Above) The new Scarlet Characin, *Cheirodon axelrodi*, spawns exactly like the Neon Tetra. (Below) The Congo Tetra.

(Above) The Tetra from Buenos Aires, *Hemigrammus caudovitattus*, a large Tetra favorite. (Below) The "one-lined" Pencil Fish.

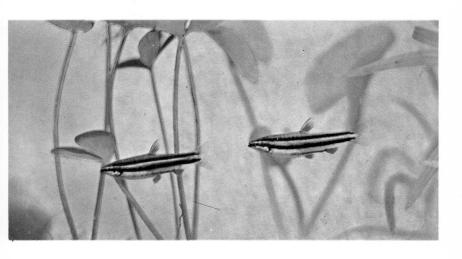

(Above) *Anostomus anostomus.* (Below) Egyptian mouthbreeder.

The Black Ruby Barb, *Puntius nigrofasciatus* Gunther

In its spawning colors, this Barb is second to none in the Barb family. As with the others, the male has the lion's share of the bright hues. Native to Ceylon, this is one of the medium-sized Barbs, which does not exceed 2½ inches in length. The male's body is suffused with a deep, cherry red at spawning time, and there are 3 broad black bars on the sides, which extend into the dorsal and anal fins. The scales each carry a golden dot, and the head is purple in color. The female has the bars, but the deep red of the male is only palely reflected here.

Breeding is the same as for the Rosy Barb, but the pair should be well conditioned and in the best of health.

The Checkered Barb, *Puntius oligolepis* Bleeker
(See color photo on page 65.)

The large, shining scales and attractive colors of this perky little Barb make it an attractive addition to any collection. Native to Sumatra, it barely reaches a length of 2 inches. The back is olive green; there are two horizontal rows of alternating black and light scales. Each light scale is topped by a dark scale, giving a checkerboard pattern. The male's fins are a brownish red, edged with black; the female has light brown fins and less body color.

This peaceful little fish has the added attraction of being very easily bred. Standard procedure as for the other small Barbs is followed.

The Half-Striped Barb, *Puntius semifasciolatus* Gunther

Very few fishes come from China, but this is one of them. Its length of 2½ inches makes it one of the smaller ones. Color is an olive green with a slight golden tinge, and the fins are reddish. There are several irregular narrow black bars which extend from the back half-way down the sides. It is easily spawned, like the others.

The Golden or Brocaded Barb, *Puntius sachsi* Ladiges

This very attractive fish was at first believed to be a golden sport of the preceding species. The body color is bright gold, with red fins. There is a vertical black bar at the tail base, and several irregular black patches appear on the body. It is prolific, and peaceful as well.

The Cherry Barb, *Puntius titteya* Deraniyagala
(See color photo on page 65.)

This is another of the popular small Barbs, which comes from southern India and Ceylon. In size it barely attains 2 inches, and in disposition it is peaceful. A broad black horizontal line characterizes both sexes, and another golden line borders it on top. The male has a brown back, and below the black line has a reddish ventral region, which becomes brilliant cherry red at spawning time. Fins and tail are also red. The female is chocolate brown on the sides, with a silvery belly and little or no color in the fins.

The species is prolific and easy to spawn in the regular manner for small Barbs.

The Sumatran or Tiger Barb, *Puntius tetrazona* Bleeker

Although the name of this popular Barb was corrected many years ago, dealers and hobbyists everywhere still refer to it as "Barbus sumatranus." It is by far the most showy member of the family, which accounts for its widespread acclaim. Body length is usually under 2 inches, and the habitat is Borneo and Thailand. This fish is sometimes guilty of nipping an occasional fin, and it would be unwise to keep it in the company of such long-finned species as the Angelfish or any of the Gourami family.

The short, stocky body is silvery in color, with a light rosy tinge. Four wide black vertical bars cross the body; the first one passes through the eye, and the second halfway between the head and the dorsal fin. The third comes down from a point just behind the dorsal fin, and extends into the anal fin, and the fourth is at the base of the tail. The dorsal fin is a thing of beauty: black, with a red edge and a narrow streak of white between. The male's nose is cherry red. The female's colors are only slightly less intense, but her greater girth identifies her easily.

The *P. tetrazona* is readily bred, using the same methods as for the other medium-sized Barbs.

Stoliczka's Barb, *Puntius stoliczkai* Day

In color, this fish resembles a small facsimile of the Rosy Barb. The black spot toward the tail is a bit larger in relation to the overall size of 2½ inches, and there is another spot behind the gill plate. Instead of being black, the dorsal fin is yellow, with a red border. It is native to Burma and Thailand, and may be bred like the others.

Genus *Rasbora*

The Harlequin Fish or Rasbora, *Rasbora heteromorpha* Duncker

Although there are many species of *Rasbora*, this particular species is so much better known than others that it is usually called simply "Rasbora." German hobbyists call this one "Keilfleckbarbe", which means "wedge-spot Barb."

These Rasbora are native to Sumatra, Malaya and Thailand and are so common that they are used for food in Singapore, despite their sardine-like size of 2 inches. In an aquarium, they leave nothing to be desired: they are peaceful and colorful. They have an unusual velvety black triangle against a red background on the posterior half of the body. The anterior half has a violet iridescence. With red dorsal and tail fins, the *R. heteromorpha* is one of the most handsome of the smaller aquarium fishes.

Spawning this little beauty is not the easiest of tasks. A tank of 5 gallons capacity should be provided, and stocked with some wide-leaved plants. Their native water has been found to be soft and strongly acid so the water should be less than 5 degrees in hardness, and the pH value should read about 6.2. A combination of distilled water and the bark extract recommended for the Neon Tetra would be a means of arriving at the proper water values. A well-conditioned pair is added, and the water brought to 78°. If all goes well, the male will, after a pretty courtship, lure the female under one of the broad leaves, where both will assume an upside-down position and deposit the eggs there. The parents are removed when they have finished. The eggs hatch the next day, and the fry are easily raised by the usual feeding methods once they begin to swim.

The Dwarf Rasbora, *Rasbora maculata* Duncker

This is the smallest member of the family, and is fully grown when 1 inch long. Because of its small size, it is best to keep these little fellows by themselves in order to meet their water requirements and thus to see the colors at their very brightest.

They are yellow with black caudal, anal and shoulder spots. Water requirements are the same as for *R. heteromorpha,* and the tank may be planted in the same manner. Condition the breeders separately until the female is bulging with eggs, then add them to the breeding tank on an evening when you expect the next morning to be sunny. Place the tank where it will get a little sunlight in the morning, and you can be reasonably sure of success. Temperature should be 78°, and spawning is accomplished in a similar manner to *R. heteromorpha*. The fry are quite easily raised.

Genus *Tanichthys*

The White Cloud Mountain Fish, *Tanichthys albonubes* Lin

Here we have another fish from China. Since its introduction in 1932, it has been a favorite of fanciers the world over. A small fish, its maximum size is 1½ inches, and the slender body resembles the *Brachydanio* species. The body is deep blue on the back, with a golden stripe on the side, followed by a blue one below and a silvery belly. The tail has a red area in the middle, and the dorsal fin is red with a blue edge.

This is probably the easiest of all egg-laying fishes to breed;

a well-fed pair in a well-planted aquarium will produce great numbers of offspring, and seldom eat them unless pressed by hunger. The horizontal blue stripe in the youngsters is very bright, and they look very much like Neon Tetras. This species comes from slightly cooler waters than most of our tropicals, and a temperature of 70° is ample for them.

Family *Cyprinodontidae*

The family of Minnows comes under this heading. It is a huge one, and includes some of our most colorful aquarium fishes.

The Blue Gularis, *Aphyosemion gulare caeruleum* Boulenger
(*See color photo on page 70.*)

The aristocrat of the *Aphyosemion* family is this beauty. It comes from the Niger delta to the Cameroon River, in Africa. A large fish, 5½ inches long when fully grown, it may cause trouble if kept in a community tank with smaller fishes. A 10-gallon tank is sufficient for a pair. They should be provided with soft, acid water with an addition of salt as for *A. australe.*

The ground color of the male is blue, and the forward half of the body is covered with purple spots. Going back to the tail, there is a series of irregular vertical dark bars on a bright blue background. The dorsal and anal fins are blue, with purple edges. The real feature is the tail, which has a triple point. The upper half is a light blue, and the area from the middle down is bright orange, edged on the bottom with deep blue. Females have a muddy greenish color, with colorless fins, and a few purple dots.

Genus *Aplocheilus*

Panchax lineatus, *Aplocheilus lineatus* Cuvier and Valenciennes
(*See color photo on page 67.*)

This colorful Panchax comes from India and Ceylon, and is one of the larger members of the family. It is pike-like in form, and has the similar habit of not annoying anything it cannot swallow whole. Therefore it may be kept with other fishes, so long as they are not small. The male may be recognized by a series of purplish horizontal stripes which run the length of his body. The dorsal and anal fins are green, edged with bright red, and the green tail also has a red stripe on the top and bottom. The ventral fins are somewhat elongated. The female has a green body, and a series of dark vertical bars, which makes her easy to distinguish.

Family *Centrarchidae*

This is the family of Basses, Perches and Sunfishes which is familiar to all fresh-water fishermen. Some of the Sunfishes may be kept in aquaria, but because of their rather pugnacious nature, most of them are not entirely satisfactory. There is one worth mentioning, however.

The Black-Banded Sunfish, *Mesogonistius chaetodon* **Baird**

German aquarists place a much higher value on the Black-Banded Sunfish than most aquarists in this country do. It is found from southern New Jersey to northern Florida, and does not exceed 3 inches. The body is silvery, peppered with black. Distinguishable through this peppering are 6 to 8 vertical black bars. The ventral fins are black, edged with orange. The species is quite peaceful and very attractive.

Spawning is performed in the usual Sunfish manner: a depression is dug in the sand, and the eggs laid into it by the female, to be immediately followed by the male, who fertilizes them. The female is then driven away, and the male fans and guards the eggs until they hatch, at which time other depressions are dug and the young shifted around until they are able to swim. At this time the male should be removed, and feeding begun with newly hatched Brine Shrimp.

Family *Gobiidae*

The Bumblebee Fish, *Brachygobius nunus* Gunther
(See color photo on page 68.)

This interesting little fellow is only 1½ inches in length, and comes from Malaya. Its body is yellow, with 4 black vertical bands which make it resemble an underwater bumblebee.

They spawn like Cichlids, using a flowerpot laid on its side. Eggs take 5 days to hatch, and are guarded by the male.

Family *Characidae*

The fishes in this group number far more than a thousand species. Most of them come from South America, and some from Africa. They are popular among aquarists because most of them are small, and many are strikingly beautiful.

The Characins, as these fishes are usually called, are egglayers and their breeding habits are diversified. In most cases eggs are deposited haphazardly among plant thickets, where the parents will eat most of them if not removed after spawning is completed. However, this is generalizing; individual spawning habits are discussed when the fish is described. Some habits are unique.

The Bloodfin, Aphyocharax rubropinnis Pappenheim

This popular little fish comes to us from Argentina. Its slender body does not exceed 2 inches in length. As the name indicates, its fins are deep red, and the rest of the fish is light blue. These fish are peaceful, but are excellent jumpers and their tank should be kept constantly covered. The female is a bit heavier-bodied than the male, and has slightly less color in her fins.

To spawn them, prepare a tank with the bottom covered with pebbles or glass marbles. Water should be slightly alkaline, and shallow, and the temperature around 75°. No plants are required. When spawning commences, there is much chasing and jumping, and the non-adhesive eggs fall to the bottom among the pebbles, where the parents have trouble finding them afterwards. The sooner you remove the parents when spawning is complete, the more eggs you will have. Hatching is completed in 36 hours, and the fry are easily raised on dust-fine foods.

Genus *Carnegiella*

The Black-Winged Hatchet Fish, *Carnegiella marthae* Myers

Dr. George S. Myers, who named this fish, must have thought very highly of it; he named it after his wife.

The Hatchet Fishes are among the more oddly-shaped fishes in this group; they have a keeled belly and huge pectoral fins. *C. marthae* is the smallest member of the family, and probably the easiest to keep. As these fish are top-feeders, probably jumping out of the water for insects in their natural habitat, this diet is not an easy one to duplicate. They are fond of swatted flies. You can train them to take floating dried foods, however. Breeding them is still an accomplishment which has not been realized. Keep their tank covered, or you are likely to find them in another tank or on the floor.

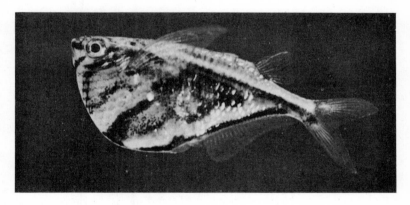

The Marbled Hatchet Fish, *Carnegiella vesca*

The Marbled Hatchet Fish is a bit larger than its preceding cousin, attaining 2 inches to *C. marthae's* 1½ inches. Both come from the Guianas and the Amazon Basin. The mottled pattern of wavy lines on a mother-of-pearl body distinguishes the *C. strigata* from all the other Hatchet Fishes. Habits are similar, and this beauty has never been spawned either.

Genus *Chilodus*

The Spotted Head-Stander, *Chilodus punctatus* Muller and Troschel

This silvery, black-spotted fish comes from the Guianas, and is somewhat high in price; the reason for this is twofold. First, the fish is a bit delicate, and must be handled as little as possible. Second, this species has seldom if ever been bred in captivity and so all stock is imported. If there were some tank-bred stock to work with, the fish might prove more hardy and easier to breed. Sexes are difficult to distinguish. If they filled up with eggs, the female would show the rounder body; a ripe female, however, is a rare sight. The body length attains 4 inches, and the disposition is peaceful. A peculiarity is the usual head-down swimming position, for which there seems to be no reason.

Genus *Copeína*

The Splash Tetra, *Copeína arnoldí* Regan

Here we have a fish with one of the strangest breeding habits. It comes from Venezuela, ranging northward to the Amazon River. The slender body is full-grown at 3 inches, and the colors range from chocolate brown on the back to blue-spotted sides and a yellowish belly. There is a black spot in the dorsal fin of both sexes, but the male can easily be distinguished by his long, pointed fins.

For breeding, a 15-gallon aquarium with neutral to slightly acid water is kept at a temperature of 75° to 78°. The water is brought to within 3 inches of the top, and the tank covered with a pane of glass. A strip of frosted glass about 4 inches wide and preferably green in color is slipped under the cover glass so that it extends across the tank near the middle.

If they are ready for spawning, the pair will show great interest in this strip of darker glass, and eventually both will leap up and assume an upside-down side-by-side position under the frosted glass, at the same time releasing a mass of sticky eggs which cling to the glass. This process is repeated until the female is depleted. The male then takes charge, swimming under the eggs at intervals and splashing water upwards so that they remain wet. This goes on for 3 days until the fry emerge and fall into the water. The parents may then be removed, and the youngsters raised in the usual manner.

The Beautiful-Scaled Characin, *Copeina callolepis* Regan

This fish is only occasionally available. Although it resembles its cousin *C. arnoldi* a great deal, it is distinguished by rows of black dots on the sides. Spawning is much different, however. Eggs are usually placed on the broad submerged leaf of a plant. This fish is often mistakenly sold as *C. arnoldi* by dealers.

The Red-Spotted Copeina, *Copeina guttata* Steindachner

The Red-Spotted Copeina does not resemble the other two, either in appearance or habits. Its body is considerably heavier, and it grows to about 4 inches in length. Oddly enough, wild specimens grow to only 3 inches; this is the only instance of a fish growing larger in captivity than in its natural environment. The coloring is attractive, a steel-blue body with red dots in horizontal rows, and yellowish red fins. The female lacks the red dots. Another oddity is that this fish spawns somewhat like our Sunfish. It scoops out a depression in the gravel on the bottom and deposits the eggs in it. For 48 hours the male guards them but he should be removed when the eggs hatch. Fry are easily raised.

Genus *Gasteropelecus*

The Silver Hatchet Fish, *Gasteropelecus levis* Eigenmann

Like the other Hatchet Fishes, this one is attractive and oddly shaped. The body has the same deep keel, and the entire fish is silvery, with the exception of a black horizontal line. It comes from the Amazon basin, attains a size of 2½ inches, and has never been bred in captivity. It is not one of the hardiest fishes to keep.

Genus *Gymnocorymbus*

The Black Tetra, *Gymnocorymbus ternetzi* Boulenger

Paraguay is the home of this favorite. It is one of the larger Tetras, attaining a length of 3 inches. When large, they may cause some trouble if kept in a community aquarium with smaller fishes.

Young specimens are especially attractive, with the posterior half of the body a deep black. This gradually fades to a gray as the fish gets older. The males are slimmer and smaller than the heavier-bodied females.

Breeding is easily accomplished if the sexes have been separated and well conditioned. The breeding aquarium should be at least 10 gallons in capacity; 15 or even 20 gallons is even better, because spawnings are large. Water should be partly fresh and nearly neutral, and there should be plenty of bushy plants. At about 78°, driving will begin, the female often taking the initiative. Eggs are scattered all over the plants, and the parents should be removed immediately after spawning is completed. Fry should be given adequate feedings as soon as they become free-swimming.

· The Glow-Light Tetra, *Hemigrammus gracilis* Reinhardt

This peaceful Tetra made its appearance in this country at about the same time as the famous Neon Tetra, and has shared its popularity. It attains a length of 1¾ inches, and is characterized by a glowing red line through the center of the body which resembles nothing so much as a lighted neon tube. The male is considerably more slender than the female.

Water for spawning this fish should be slightly acid and quite soft. At a temperature of 78° to 80°, the pair will soon be observed swimming closely together into the plants, which should not be too closely bunched. Here they lock fins and do a sort of "barrel roll," at the same time expelling a few eggs, some of which fall to the bottom. After the spawning is completed, the aquarium should be covered to shade it until the fry hatch; this takes place in about 48 hours. Parents should of course be removed when their work of spawning is done.

The Golden Tetra, *Hemigrammus armstrongi* Schultz and Axelrod

This attractive little fish looks as if it had been dipped in gold. It is native to British Guiana, and only 1½ inches in length. Sexes cannot be distinguished by color, but the females have the deeper, heavier body. They have a peaceful, rather shy disposition.

Breeding is similar to the Black Tetra, but a smaller tank may be used.

The Head-and-Tail-Light, *Hemigrammus ocellifer* Steindachner

This is one of the old perennials among tropical aquarium favorites. It is a sturdy, good-looking Tetra which is easily kept and bred. There is a bright red spot at the top of the tail base, which is matched by the upper half of the eye. When lighted from above, it looks as if it had lights glowing fore and aft. Males can be distinguished by a white spot in the anal fin.

Spawning is done in a manner similar to the Black Tetra but a smaller tank may be used, about 3 to 5 gallons in capacity. For almost sure-fire results, the German breeders gather enough rainwater to fill the tank and then stir in a handful of whitewash. This mixture is allowed to settle and clear over a period of a few days. Then the clear water is siphoned off, and is ready for immediate use. The Head-and-Tail-Lights may be added, and if they are in good condition will spawn almost at once. When they are finished, remove them and shade the tank with newspaper or a towel. Three days later you will be able to see the fry hanging on the glass and plants, and you may discontinue the shading. Begin feeding in the usual manner when the youngsters begin to swim.

The Pretty Tetra, *Hemigrammus pulcher* Ladiges

This Tetra comes from the Peruvian Amazon, and does not have the compressed body characteristic of the other *Hemigrammus* species. It is short and heavy-bodied, and has a rectangular black spot which extends from the tail base to almost the middle of the body. There is an orange spot at the top of the tail base, and the upper half of the eye is red.

A well-conditioned pair will spawn in the same manner as the Black Tetra, if the female is heavy with eggs. Size may be up to 2 inches, but most specimens are a bit smaller.

The Rummy-Nosed Tetra, *Hemigrammus rhodostomus* Ahl

Unfortunately this handsome fish from Brazil does not spawn readily. Breeding this fish is an accomplishment that can be claimed by only a few aquarists, who seem to have succeeded by conditioning their breeding pairs with live daphnia, and using soft, slightly acid water.

Identification of this fish is easy. The body is a bit more elongated than the usual *Hemigrammus*. Body color is silvery, with a large black area at the tail base which narrows to a point at the fork of the tail. The tail lobes are crossed in the center by a black stripe, and the black area at the tail base narrows down to a line which extends about three-quarters of the way toward the head. The bibulous name is derived from the bright red area which covers the nose.

The Feather Fin, *Hemigrammus unilineatus* Gill

The Feather Fin resembles the Head-and-Tail-Light a great deal in body form. The difference is that the bright spots are lacking, but the dorsal fin is adorned with a black spot, and the anal fin is edged with black. The female of this species is considerably heavier than the male, and sexes are easy to distinguish in mature pairs.

The same method given for spawning the Head-and-Tail-Light may also be used for this fish.

The Flame Tetra (Tetra from Rio)

The Flame Tetra or Tetra from Rio, *Hyphessobrycon flammeus* Myers
(See photo on opposite page.)

This is another old favorite. It has everything to recommend it: color, peaceful disposition, hardiness, and ease of breeding. It rarely attains a length of 2 inches; most adult specimens are nearer 1½ inches. The posterior half of the body is a bright red, as are the dorsal, tail, anal and ventral fins. Two short black bars adorn the sides in the front half of the body. The male is easily distinguished by the fact that his anal fin and the front half of the dorsal are edged with black.

Breeding is the same as for the Black Tetra, but smaller aquaria may be used.

The Neon Tetra, *Hyphessobrycon innesi* Myers

Probably no other aquarium fish has caused the excitement that this one did when it was first introduced. It was first discovered by Auguste Rabaut in the Peruvian headwaters of the Amazon River about 20 years ago. Rabaut sent some specimens to Paris, whence some traveled to Germany; some were then transported to this country via the dirigible "Hindenburg," shortly before its tragic crash.

Aquarists who were fortunate enough to get them tried to spawn them but most efforts were unsuccessful. The few lucky ones were the very ones who were able to breed *Rasbora hetero-morpha,* for a similar set of water conditions is required: soft, slightly acid water. As soon as this was known, breeders everywhere took the cue and began to have results. This is not to say that the Neon Tetra is an easy fish to breed; it is still one of the so-called "problem fishes," but most of the difficulty has been removed. This is how it is done:

Use an all-glass aquarium of rectangular shape and a capacity of 1½ to 2 gallons, thoroughly cleaned and rinsed. Shave off some pieces of oak or elm bark and boil them in distilled water for about 15 minutes. The result will be a highly acid concentrate. Fill the aquarium with distilled water, and add the concentrate until the pH reading drops from 7.0 to 6.5. The remaining concentrate may be bottled for future use. Then take a quart of water and stir in one teaspoonful of powdered alum.

Take a bunch or two of bushy plants and sterilize them by letting them soak in this mixture for 5 minutes. Wash them off in clean water and place in the breeding tank. Do not use any gravel; it is not necessary and can easily cause trouble by hardening the water. The plants may be anchored with a lead strip, or a piece of glass rod. Let the breeding tank stand until the water is crystal clear.

Select a pair which is in good health, the male active and the female heavy with eggs. Do not feed them while they are in the breeding tank; if there is no spawning action within three days, take them out and try with another pair if you have them; if not, feed them well for several days and then try again. Give the tank a place which does not get any direct sunlight; when the fish have spawned, take out the parents and cover the tank for three days. By this time the fry are free-swimming, and no longer sensitive to light. For the first few days you may feed the youngsters by taking the yolk of a hard-boiled egg, placing it in a square of cloth and giving it a few squeezes while sloshing it around in the water. (Don't overdo it lest you foul the water.) When the fry have grown somewhat, switch to freshly-hatched brine shrimp.

Body size of this slender fish is 1½ inches. The upper half of the body, from the eye almost to the tail, is brilliant greenish blue. The belly is white, and the lower posterior half of the body is bright red. Females have a slightly deeper body.

The Lemon Tetra, *Hyphessobrycon pulchripinnis* Ahl

From the Amazon basin comes this attractive member of the Characin family. This fish in the bare tanks of a dealer seems almost colorless, but this is not the case when it is tranferred to a planted aquarium, where it becomes a thing of beauty. The body length is 1¾ inches when fully grown. There is a streak of lemon yellow in the upper half of the dorsal fin, as well as the front edge of the anal fin, which is further adorned with a black streak behind it, and a black edge. The eye is a brilliant red. Females have a deeper body and slightly less color.

Spawning is similar to that of the Black Tetra (p. 98).

The Black-Lined Tetra, *Hyphessobrycon scholzei* Ahl

This is one of the larger Tetras, which grows to about 3 inches in length. It is a silvery fish, with a prominent black horizontal line crossing the body from the gill-plate to the tail, where it ends in a triangular spot. The female is considerably deeper-bodied than the male.

These fish are easily propagated in the same manner as the Black Tetra. They are so hardy that it is possible for the breeders in Florida to raise them in huge quantities the year round in pools.

The Jewel Tetra, *Hyphessobrycon callistus* Boulenger
(*See color photo on page 72.*)

There has been a certain amount of confusion connected with the naming of this fish. It seems to vary in color in its rather wide-ly distributed haunts, and has been known as *H. serpae* and *H. minor,* depending on its local colors. Some specimens show a brilliant red color, and others are much more subdued. This refers to body color; the tail and anal fins are bright red in all, and the dorsal fin is almost all black. There is a narrow vertical black streak on the side a short way behind the gill-plate, and the anal fin is tipped with black and edged with white, as are the ventral fins. This fish is fully grown at 1½ inches.

Spawning is similar to the procedure for the black Tetra (p. 98).

The Rosy Tetra, *Hyphessobrycon rosaceus* Durbin
(See color photo on page 72.)

The first thing you notice about this fish is the large, showy dorsal fin of the male. Native to the lower Amazon and British Guiana, it reaches a size of 1¾ inches. The body is a bit deeper than most members of this family, and healthy specimens have a rosy tint. The ventral and anal fins, as well as the outer edges of the tail are bright red, and the dorsal fin carries a large black area with white margins. The male's dorsal fin is about twice as long as that of his mate, making it an easy task to distinguish him.

It is easily bred in the same manner as the Black Tetra.

Genus Nannostomus

The One-Lined Pencil Fish, *Nannostomus marginatus* Eigenmann
(See color photo on page 79.)

British Guiana is the home of this, the smallest of the Pencil Fishes. Its size is only 1½ inches, and at first glance the name "one-lined" seems like a misnomer. There is one golden line, bordered above and below by wide black lines. The belly is white, and the dorsal, anal and ventral fins are deep red.

This little fish requires something in addition to the usual procedure for spawning. Water level should be brought down to about 3 inches, and the bottom covered with a layer of pebbles or glass marbles. The parents are very fond of their own eggs, and would surely eat them all if they could. However, some eggs fall between the pebbles, where they are inaccessible.

The Golden Pencil Fish, *Nannostomus anomalus* Steindachner

The name "Pencil Fish" has been applied to this family because of the elongated body structure and pointed snout. They are peaceful and colorful, but in a community aquarium there is a possibility that they may not get their fair share of food because of their leisurely manner of swimming. The Golden Pencil Fish comes from the basin of the Amazon and the Rio Negro. It attains 2 inches in length; the back is brown, and there is a bright golden band which runs the full length of the body, bordered below by a wide black band. The belly is white, and the ventral and anal fins of the male have white tips.

Spawning temperature seems to be best at about 78°. Soft water which is slightly acid is best, and bushy plants like *Myriophyllum* should occupy about half of a 5-gallon tank. Eggs hatch in about 48 hours, and the young require very fine foods at first.

Genus *Pristella*

Pristella riddlei Meek

German fanciers call these "water-finches," but there has never been a popular name for them in this country, although they are just as popular here. They come from Eastern Venezuela, the Orinoco Basin and the Guianas, and 2 inches is their extreme length, although most specimens are no more than 1½ inches long. They are graceful and well-proportioned, and a small school of them is an attractive addition to any aquarium. The back is brown, and there is an indistinct horizontal line. The belly is silvery, and there is a spot on the dorsal, anal and ventral fins; the tail is rosy pink. The female is considerably heavier in body than the male.

If you desire to breed this fish, make sure that you have a mature pair to work with. This means a pair of fish which is more than a year old, as they grow rather slowly. Use a tank of about 5 gallons capacity, and water which is about neutral. The usual bushy plants and a well-conditioned pair complete the picture. They spawn in the usual Tetra fashion. Temperature should be kept at about 80°.

Genus *Phenacogrammus*

The Congo Tetra, *Phenacogrammus interruptus* Boulenger
(*See color photo on page 78.*)

One of the most beautiful Tetras to reach our shores in recent years is this one. It comes from the upper Congo River, and is one of the larger members of the family. Its full-grown length slightly exceeds 3 inches and, although it is peaceful in the community tank, it is best to keep it away from small fishes. This is a good rule for all community aquaria.

In order to appreciate this lovely fish fully, and also to keep it in good health with the possibility of spawning it, you must take cognizance of its special requirements. In the first place you need a large aquarium, at least 15 gallons in capacity. The water must be soft—no more than 6 degrees of hardness. The water must also be acid, with a pH value of about 6.5. This is the same water which is recommended for the Neon Tetra but the use of 15 gallons of distilled water may be expensive. Rain water could be used after aging; if the acidity is lacking, the bark extract mentioned in the section on Neon Tetras can be used, or else the water may be filtered through peat moss until the proper acidity is reached.

A healthy pair of *Phenacogrammus interruptus* with the sun shining on them is a breath-taking sight; their large scales gleam in all the iridescent colors of the rainbow, with the accent on blues and violets. The fins are blue; the male has the larger dorsal and anal fins, and his tail has several elongated rays in the center, which stream out beyond the lobes. Spawning, if you are lucky, is performed in the usual Tetra fashion, and the parents should be removed afterward and the tank darkened for 3 days.

Family *Cichlidae*

The Cichlids are another very large family which includes many aquarium fishes. Some have the drawback of being rather vicious, but all are interesting in their breeding habits; they are usually devoted parents, lavishing extreme affection on their young, but at times, for no apparent reason, they make a meal of them.

Space forbids a complete listing, but the ones chosen are representative of the rest.

Genus *Aequidens*

The Blue Acara, *Aequidens pulcher* Gill

One of the large Cichlids, the Blue Acara sometimes attains a length of 6 inches, although most specimens are somewhat smaller. It may be kept with larger fishes, but would prove a bit "rough" with small fishes in a community aquarium. The body is marked with 8 or 9 vertical bars, and the fish is peppered all over with blue spots.

Spawning is usually quite easy to induce. A large aquarium of at least 20 gallons is required, with gravel and a few rocks in it. Separate the breeders for a time, until the female is heavy with roe, then place the pair in the tank. When they have become accustomed to their surroundings, the male begins to clean off one of the rocks. When this job is done to their mutual satisfaction, the female begins to glide over the rock. As her vent touches it, she releases a row of eggs which adhere there. The male follows just behind and fertilizes the eggs. Row after row of eggs are laid and fertilized. The male usually takes charge of guarding them, although the female sometimes guards them too. When the eggs hatch, the parents dig holes in the gravel and move the young about. When the fry become free-swimming, they are constantly herded until such time as they revolt against this parental supervision. By this time the parents are often ready to spawn again. Brine shrimp or sifted Daphnia should be provided when the fry begin to swim; the best food for the parents is cut-up garden worms or some other form of worm food.

Genus *Pterophyllum*

The Angelfish, *Pterophyllum eimekei* Ahl
(See color photo on page 71.)

There is something about the way an Angelfish moves that appeals to all who watch this most dignified of aquarium fish. It comes from the Rio Negro and Amazon Basin and attains a size of 5 inches. It has 4 vertical bands on a silvery body, and the dorsal is as high as the diameter of the body. The anal fin is the same length, with a long ray which extends back much further. The ventral fins consist only of a few rays, one of which is also very much elongated. The first and last rays of the tail fin are extended as well. The eye is red.

Eggs are laid Cichlid-fashion, usually on the leaf of a large plant. Parental care is divided, and a well-mated pair will seldom eat their young, from which they should be removed as soon as they begin to swim.

An all-black variety has been developed which promises to

become one of the most popular aquarium fishes when it is generally available.

Genus *Symphysodon*

The Discus, *Symphysodon discus* Heckel
(See color photo on page 71.)

This beauty is hard to feed, hard to keep and almost impossible to breed. The body is shaped like a pancake stood on end, and attains a diameter of 9 inches. The main color is brown, and there are 9 vertical bars. The fins are blue, mottled with bright red. The male has some of these blue and red markings in the back and belly regions as well. The ventral fins are edged with bright red.

They spawn in a very similar manner to the Angelfish, whose habitat they share. A few breeders are producing them at present; it is hoped that succeeding generations will be a bit easier to handle.

Genus *Cichlasoma*

The Flag Cichlid, *Cichlasoma festivum* Heckel

This is one of the really peaceful Cichlids, although it is a large one which sometimes grows to 6 inches. Its mark of distinction is an oblique line which begins at the mouth, travels upward through the eye, and ends at the tip of the dorsal fin. There are indistinct vertical bars, and a black spot at the tail base which is ringed with yellow.

The Fire-Mouth Cichlid, *Cichlasoma meeki* Brind
(See color photo on page 75.)

There is no mistaking this large Cichlid: a fiery red area extends from the chin through the entire belly. The body is dark brown, with indistinct vertical bars and a horizontal line which ends in a large black spot in the middle of the body. There is another black spot in the red area at the bottom of the gill-plate. The male has the more pointed dorsal fin. This fish comes from Yucatan. A word of warning: this fish should not be kept in a community aquarium with smaller fishes. It is safe only in the company of big fellows like itself.

It breeds like the Blue Acara.

The Banded Cichlid, or Convict Fish, *Cichlasoma severum* Heckel
(See color photo on page 75.)

The word "banded" is an accurate description of the fish only when it is half-grown. By the time maturity is attained, the bands have practically faded out. Only one band remains, running from the base of the dorsal fin to the base of the anal fin and ending in a spot on each end. This is one of the big Cichlids, and should be treated accordingly. It is 6 inches long and heavy-bodied, so give it a large aquarium; 30 gallons is not too big. The sides are a light brown with a greenish tinge, covered with red spots. The fins are reddish, and covered with blue spots. The female is much duller in color, and her fins are shorter.

It comes from the Guianas, Rio Negro and the Amazon Basin, and breeds like the Blue Acara.

Genus *Apistogramma*

The Agassiz Dwarf Cichlid, *Apistogramma agassizi* Steindachner

This is referred to as a "dwarf," being 3 inches in length at most. The shape of the tail is an easy means of identification: it comes to a single point. Body color is a yellowish brown. There is a black horizontal line from the mouth to the tip of the tail, and the fins are blue, edged with red. The female has plain round

fins, and is a bit more yellow in body color. It is native to the Amazon Basin.

Breeding is similar to that of the Blue Acara, but a much smaller aquarium may be used; 5 gallons is sufficient. There is one important difference, however: after spawning, the little female begins to attack her much bigger mate, and may injure or even kill him if he is left with her. He should be removed, and the female will take over all parental duties herself.

Ramirez's Dwarf Cichlid, *Apistogramma ramirezi* Myers Harry
(*See color photo on page 73.*)

German aquarists call this one the "Butterfly Cichlid." Its body color is blue, and there are a number of brown vertical bars, especially noticeable in the female. The body is sprinkled with gleaming light-blue spots. The high, saddle-shaped dorsal fin is blue, edged with orange, and the first rays are black. These first rays are elongated in the male. Large specimens sometimes attain 3 inches, but most are a bit smaller.

A temperature of 80° is recommended for their breeding, and they follow the procedure of the preceding species. They are a bit timid, however, and are apt to eat their eggs. Dense planting may help somewhat.

Genus *Pelmatochromis*

Pelmatochromis kribensis Boulenger
(See color photo on page 73.)

This visitor from the Congo River in Africa has not been with us long enough to get a popular name, but there is no question of its popularity. Top size for males is about 3 inches while females fall short of this mark by about an inch. They behave well in a community aquarium, and are very colorful. The upper part of the male's body is dark blue, and a horizontal stripe crosses the body from mouth to tail. The lower part of the body is lighter, and a large region about the belly is wine-red. The upper part of the tail has two, three or even four black dots ringed with yellow, and the dorsal fin of the male carries one dot. The female has only one dot on the tail, and two on the dorsal fin. The anal fin of the male is violet, as are the ventral fins, which have a blue edge besides. The dorsal fin is blue, bordered with a wide gold edge which is in turn edged with red. When spawning, the female takes on a bright coppery tinge in the after half of the body, and rivals her mate in brilliance of coloration.

Spawning is tricky as they like to lay their eggs where they will be well hidden. The best spawning site with which to provide them is a flowerpot with a notch cut out of the upper edge. Set it upright in the aquarium and cover it with a piece of slate. They will soon swim in and out, and will eventually spawn there. As with the other Dwarf Cichlids, the female will usually take over the housekeeping duties. It is best to remove the male. Unfortunately, the eggs are often eaten.

Family Anabantidae

Some very interesting and colorful fishes are included in this family. The Anabantids are unusual in that they must occasionally come up for a gulp of air, and have a special breathing mechanism known as a "labyrinth" which handles this air. These fishes include such aquarium favorites as the Betta, the Gouramis, and others. Most of them make nests at the surface by blowing bubbles; the eggs are placed into these and guarded.

Genus Betta

The Siamese Fighting Fish, Betta splendens Regan
(See color photos on pages 76 and 77.)

The Siamese make use of this fish in a gambling game in their own country, where this fish comes from. The males, while not particularly vicious when alone, becames hellions when another male is placed in close quarters with them, and a good fighter, like a fighting-cock in Mexico, can be a valuable asset to its owner.

There is very little resemblance between the short-finned, not particularly colorful fish which the Siamese use and the long-finned, brightly-colored beauties which have been developed from them. The body is slender and 2½ inches long, with long, flowing tail and anal fins, and a high dorsal. Color varieties are numerous, with many combinations of blue, green, red, and a white-bodied fish with red or blue fins. There is even an albino with a white body and fins, and pink eyes. The females have shorter fins and heavier abdomens. They thrive on living foods, but can be carried over for quite a time on prepared foods also.

The breeding behavior of this fish, as well as the other members of the family, is an interesting procedure. Fill a 10-gallon aquarium to a depth of about 5 inches with water which has been aged a few days, and is about neutral. No gravel is required on the bottom, and there is no need for plants. First place the male in the tank. When he signifies his willingness to spawn by blowing a mass of bubbles, introduce a female whose abdomen is bulging. After many tries, the male will lure her under the bubbles, where he wraps his body around hers and squeezes a few eggs out of her, which he fertilizes at the same time. This act is repeated over and over, until the female is depleted, at which time she is driven away. The male then takes full charge of the bubble-nest, and the female should be taken out. In about 30 to 40 hours the eggs hatch, and the male keeps busy retrieving fry which fall out of the nest to the bottom. When the fry become free-swimming, they leave the nest and begin to search for food, at which time the male's work is done, and he should be removed. Dust-fine foods may be fed at this time, to be followed by freshly hatched Brine Shrimp, which the youngsters soon learn to tear to pieces with their sharp teeth.

Genus *Colisa*

The Dwarf Gourami, *Colisa lalia* Hamilton-Buchanan
(See color photo on page 74.)

Probably the best-known of the Gouramis is the Dwarf Gourami. It is a small fish, the male about 2 inches in length, and the females slightly smaller. They are native to India, and are a peaceful species. As is usual with fishes, the male comes in for the lion's share of the colors. There are alternating slanting vertical bars of bright blue and red which pass through the entire length of the body, and the fins are orange, sprinkled with red. At spawning time, the region from the chin to the belly is suffused with bright deep blue. The female has pale bars and plain fins. The ventral fins are unique: they consist of one long ray, which is very flexible. These fins are used as "feelers" and the fish touches everything within range with them.

Breeding is the same as for the Betta, except that these fish like to weave some plant leaves into their nest so a few floating plants are welcome.

Genus *Trichogaster*

The Three-Spot or Blue Gourami, *Trichogaster trichopterus* Palas

Whoever gave this fish the name "Three-Spot Gourami" counted the eye as one spot, because there are only two spots on each side of the body. It comes from Sumatra. It grows as large as 5 inches, at which size it should be kept with large fishes only. The entire body of the male is suffused with blue, and there are many irregular wobbly vertical dark bars. The fins are a lighter blue, and covered with large white dots.

They breed like Bettas, and are easily raised.

The Pearl or Mosaic Gourami, *Trichogaster leeri* Bleeker
(*See color photo on page 74.*)

Many people consider this peaceful fish the most beautiful of all the Gouramis. It grows to 5 inches. The body is covered with a fine, reticulated pattern, and the ground color is silvery with a mother-of-pearl sheen, which often shows as a pale violet. At spawning time, the male develops an orange-red area from the chin all through the belly area. Another way to distinguish him is by the deeper anal and higher dorsal fins. Both sexes show a heavy black line which begins at the mouth and fades out about three-quarters of the way down the body.

This fish comes from Sumatra, Borneo, Malaya and Thailand, and breeds in a similar manner to the Betta.

Family *Cobitidae*

Genus *Botia*

The Clown Loach, *Botia macracanthus* Bleeker

(See color photo on page 66.)

In the comparatively few years it has become available to aquarists, the Clown Loach has become very popular, and for good reason. The body is a rich orange-red in color, with a wide black saddle crossing from just ahead of the dorsal fin to the belly, and wide black band extending from behind the dorsal fin to the anal fin. The tail and fins are bright red. Most specimens offered by dealers are 3 to 4 inches in length, but they grow much larger. Unfortunately, it is a bit of a "shrinking violet" in the daytime, being largely nocturnal in its habits. If there have ever been any successful spawnings, they were never made public.

Family *Callíchthydae*

Genus *Corydoras*

These are the Armored Catfishes, which come to us from South America; they are identified by a series of bony plates on the sides in lieu of scales. They spend their time on the bottom grubbing around for some bit of food the others missed, a habit which makes them extremely valuable to the aquarist. Not only do they clean up otherwise uneaten food, but they also keep the gravel loose around the plant roots, thereby cultivating them. Seldom is their digging vigorous enough to dislodge rooted plants.

These bony fishes require calcium, so give them slightly alkaline water in the breeding tank. Not much planting is required; most of the eggs are deposited on the glass sides. A 10-gallon aquarium is ample for all *Corydoras* species. The breeding act is interesting. The pair becomes unusually active, and chases about a great deal. Finally the male stops, and rolls over on his side. The female attaches herself to him by sucking her mouth to his belly; at the same time 4 or 5 eggs are expelled into a pocket which the female makes by pushing together her ventral fins. She then lets go and swims to a previously selected site, usually a spot on the glass sides, and first rubs the spot with her mouth, and then pushes the sticky eggs there. This process is repeated frequently. At 80°, which is the proper spawning temperature, the eggs hatch in 72 hours. The parents seldom bother their young, but there is no point in tempting them, so they should be removed. Dust-fine food should be stirred into a small jar full of water, to allow it to soak and sink to the bottom; live foods may follow when the youngsters grow.

The Arched Corydoras, *Corydoras arcuatus* Elwin

This fish is easily distinguished from the rest of the family by a wide black stripe which runs from the mouth up through the eye and along the back all the way to the bottom of the tail base. Its home is in the Amazon Basin, and size is 2½ inches. It hasn't been spawned.

The Bronze Catfish, *Corydoras aeneus* Gill

This is the most popular member of the family. The sides have a slight greenish bronze tinge, and the maximum size attained is 3 inches. Sex can be easily distinguished by looking down at them from above: the males are smaller, and the females are wider. Spawning occurs as described for the genus.

Myers' Corydoras, *Corydoras myersi* M. Ribeiro

This species is very similar to *C. arcuatus*. It has a darker, pinkish-brown body, and the wide black line, instead of curving from the mouth through the eye, starts just behind the head.

This fish breeds as described for the genus, but there is a peculiarity in the offspring: the front half of the body is red, the back half bright green and the fins are pink. As the fish grows up, the green area gradually becomes the black line, and the pink area spreads out over the lower half of the body.

The Peppered Corydoras, *Corydoras paleatus* Jenyns

This species is not seen quite as often as formerly but it is still popular. For a *Corydoras,* it is large, 4 inches. The body color is brown, and the sides are mottled with darker brown. The tail is adorned with a number of alternating light and dark vertical bars. It comes from Southern Brazil and Northern Argentina, and spawns in the manner described for the species.

The Dwarf Catfish, *Corydoras hastatus* Eigenmann

The smallest member of the family comes from the Amazon Basin. The size at maturity is 1½ inches and it is easily recognized. The body color is brown, with a horizontal stripe of black which ends in a triangular spot at the caudal base. Spawnings are numerous but small in number, and the young are not eaten

if the parents are well fed. Fry are large, and well able to fend for themselves.

The Black-Spotted Catfish, *Corydoras melanistius* Regan

This attractive Catfish comes from Venezuela. It has a pinkish body peppered with small black spots, as is the tail. The face is black, and there is a black area in the dorsal fin which extends down a little way into the body. For spawning, they require a well-planted aquarium in a spot which is partly shaded; otherwise they are inclined to be very nervous and shy.

(Above) *Nothobranchius palmquesti* comes from East Africa. (Below) These Seabats, *Monodactylus sebae*, were found in fresh water in Cameroons, Africa.

(Above) The Striped Barb, *Puntius lineatus*. (Below) *Capoeta callip-terus*, collected by Herbert R. Axelrod in Nigeria.

(Above) A small Barb, *Capoeta puckelli*, is easily spawned. (Below)
Puntius holotaenia, a Barb from Africa.

(Above) An African rarity, *Irvineia voltae*. (Below) The Nigerian Catfish, *Parauchenoglanis macrostoma*.

(Above) The Black Shark, *Labeo chrysophekadion*, from Siam. (Below) A recent import from the Far East, the Silver Gourami, *Trichogaster microlepis*.

(Above) A fairly common, though unidentified, *Aplocheilichthys* species from the Congo. (Below) *Puntius usumbarae*, a Barb from Africa.

(Above) *Aphyosemion christyi,* an African killifish. (Below) The Striped Barb from Nigeria, *Puntius chlorotaenia.*

(Above) *Ctenopoma ocellatus* is slightly different from the *Ctenopoma kingsleyae* (below). Both are African air-breathing fishes.

(Above) *Micralestes acutidens*, the Congo River silverside. (Below) *Alestes longipinnis*, a tetra from the Congo River, near Leopoldville, Belgian Congo.

(Above) The yellow-finned *Epiplatys* from the French Cameroons.
(Below) The Mirror Barb, *Puntius ablabes*, from Africa.

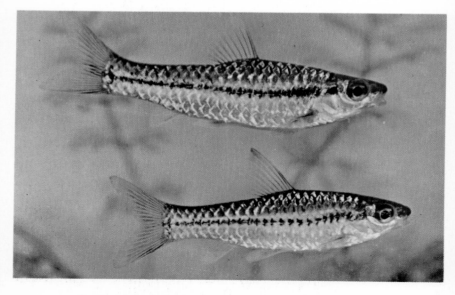

(Above) An unidentified *Aplocheilichthys* species from the Cameroons.
(Below) The Butterfly Barb from the Belgian Congo, *Capoeta hulstaerti*.

(Above) The Hockeystick, *Thayeria obliqua*, is closely related to the Penguin Fish (see page 68). (Below) An African Dwarf Cichlid, *Pelmatochromis dimidiates*.

(Above) The Egyptian Mouthbreeder, *Haplochromis multicolor*. The lower fish, the female, has a mouthful of eggs. (Below) *Steatochranes casuarius*.

These two *Epiplatys* species were collected by Herbert R. Axelrod in the French Cameroons in Africa. They are sold as *Epiplatys sexfasciatus.*

(Above) *Pelmatochromis arnoldi*, an African Dwarf Cichlid. (Below)
The Goby Cichlid, *Gobiochromis tinanti*, from the Belgian Congo.

(Above) *Distichodus fasciolatus* from Africa. (Below) The beautiful Nigerian Mouthbreeder, *Haplochromis* species, collected in Africa by Herbert R. Axelrod.